Build From Scratch

Steps, Strategies and Practical Insight into building a successful start-up enterprise

tara - india research press, new delhi

tara - india research press
B-4/22, Safdarjung Enclave
New Delhi – 110 029. India
Ph.: 24694610; Fax : 24618637
bahrisons@vsnl.com
www.indiaresearchpress.com
contact@indiaresearchpress.com

ISBN : 81-87943-43-2

Cataloguing in Publication Data
Build From Scratch
Steps, Strategies and Practical Insight
into building a successful start-up enterprise
Vineet Bajpai © 2004

1. Start-up 2. Management 3. Company
i . Title ii. Author

Printed at Focus Impressions, New Delhi – 110 003.

Build From Scratch

Steps, Strategies and Practical Insight into building a successful start-up enterprise

Acknowledgement

I often wondered why most books started with an acknowledgement section. It was only during the writing of this book that I realized the importance of these pages. I realized that although a book cover may display the name of only one author, there are many others who play an equally critical role towards the book finally reaching the readers hands. 'Build From Scratch' is no different. At a lot of places in the text I have been forced to use 'I'. I want to emphasize that every time an 'I' has been used, it should be read as salutations for the numerous people who have been my teammates and the real unsung authors of this book.

First and foremost I would like to express my gratitude to Manoj Ghai and the entire Ghai family, without whom my company, and in turn this book, would have never been possible. I thank Mr. Asheesh Khanna, who I look up to as a friend, philosopher and guide. He has unknowingly taught me more management skills than any other individual. I thank Dr. R.A. Yadav, Director – Lal Bahadur Shastri Institute of Management, New Delhi, for passing on to me few of the most heartfelt insights mentioned in this book; Mr. Praveen Puri, Director – Skyline Business School, New Delhi, for being my greatest source of academic and entrepreneurial encouragement, without whose faith I would have never been a part of the academic community.

I feel compelled to thank a lot more people who have been a constant source of encouragement throughout the writing of this book - Geetika Sinha from GE Capital International Services, Aarthi Ramakrishnan from HSBC, Vivek Merani and Prashant Misra for being my intellectual soul-mates, Munisha Nanda for being my biggest source of inspiration and Mr. Subhash and Gaurav Arora from Teksons Bookshop for being a family and guiding me at every crucial step while writing this book.

These pages would be incomplete without a mention of the Magnon Solutions Family - Nitin, Santosh, Ajay, Madhvi, Gaurav, Gurpreet, Shekhar, Vipin, Shantanu, Sudesh, Vipin, Vijay, Chiranjib, Pranab, Malika, Shashank, Manish, Philip, Rajat and Meetu – for helping me with all the big and small successes I have ever achieved.

The single most important person for the shape of this book would be none other than my elder brother Varun Bajpai for acting like a sounding board, a benchmark and the most valuable consultant for every page of the book. I would like to thank Mr. Anuj Bahri, without whose continuous interest, support and trust, this initiative could have never reached the thousands of people it intends to.

Finally, I would like to express my indebtedness to my father, Gp. Capt. DN Bajpai, for being a fantastic teacher, critic, friend and the man I hope to become one day. My mother Vandana, whose unbelievable simplicity and love are the greatest driving forces in my life.

In success and spirit,

Vineet Bajpai

Contents

Preface

How many of us are working day in and day out for some well-known organizations for years without getting the recognition we always wanted? How many of you are students who hope to hit it big in the corporate sector and in life? How many of us have actually been able to achieve all that we feel we are capable of? Why is it that even when we put in twelve hours of work everyday, we earn only enough to keep going? And why is it that some people work just the same and earn in a day what we earn in a whole year? Why is it that most of us don't even know exactly what a Mercedes E240 costs while others drive them? Why do some people buy bungalows in posh localities when most of us buy that small apartment on a loan and EMI scheme? Its just destiny, right? Absolutely wrong.

Please get me right. I do not mean to pose these questions in a negative tone. I am only trying to offer reflections of what most well-educated yet 'middle-class' people ask themselves and each other often. And the truth is that if these questions disturb you even a small bit, they do possess some harsh realities within them. Also, I am in no way trying to say that working in corporations or the government is in any way inferior when it comes to professionalism. A lot of successful people we read about in newspapers and watch on television are people who have devoted their lives to organizations to finally reach the heights they have achieved. However, we must also try and answer these economic puzzles. We must try to find out who are these people who zip past us on the roads in long cars and become darlings of the media? Who are these people who dine with ministers and film stars and head commerce and industry chambers? Almost invariably you will discover that there is a courageous and driven entrepreneur and business leader behind the picture. Someone who decided to think out-of-the-middle-class-box. A magnificent man or woman who chose to take the long tough road to glory and success over the simple 9 to 5 employment route. Someone who thought a little ahead of his or her generation. Someone who offered employment to hundreds and thousands rather than appearing for interviews every two years. Someone who broke the rules to push for the impossible. This book is like an essay and a workbook on how you can become that 'someone'.

Let us now do some deep-diving into the world of start-up businesses and entrepreneurship.

'Every thousand mile journey must begin with a single step' stated Lao-Tsu many years ago. I read this saying over ten years back but little did I know then that this would change the entire course of my professional life one day. Right from the early days of my B-school education, I developed a strong orientation towards building and managing my own enterprise and participated in long discussions with seniors, professors and colleagues on the same thought. To my disappointment, I realized that although a large number of people agreed and shared my interest, very few actually planned to go all the way and implement their ideas. The reasons were many – security of being with an established organization, stress and responsibility associated with running a business, lack of financial support, inexperience...to name some of them. And being very honest, I could identify with each one of these reasons.

I joined GE Capital International Services immediately after I completed my post graduation in Management. The experience of working with the most respected and professional company of the world played a key role in developing my understanding on a wide range of professional areas. These included critical aspects like organizational communication, team work, international perspective, quality awareness and an overall professional aptitude. As I always say, it was in that organization that I completed my management education. However, even in that environment my thirst for building my own organization remained. I would often question my managers and seniors on their views, and all of them conveyed similar opinions...but nobody was really ready to do it. It was during those days of introspection and environment scanning that something revolutionary began hitting the headlines. It was the great dot com explosion. All around me I read stories of 'magnificent men' creating history by building small models on the Internet and gathering staggering valuations. Sabeer Bhatia became a household name and Jeff Bezos was declared Time Magazine's 'Man of the Year'. Even back home .comventures were sold at mind boggling price and Indian Venture Capital companies openly declared their plans and willingness to fund Indian dot com initiatives. It was like a fairy tale for me. But before I could assess and analyze the scenario completely, the technology market took a sudden downturn. The very companies which made success stories were now declaring closure. Industry analysts were now busting the dot com business models and the scenario was getting worse with every passing day. This debacle made me understand some important issues in launching and running a business – issues of investor management, long-term revenue models and intellectual capital. (I will deal with all these issues in greater detail in the coming chapters).

It was in this bloodbath that I launched a tiny company called Magnon Solutions Pvt. Ltd. How the company was formed, how the business areas were chosen, where the financial support came from and how the infrastructure and team were built are areas I would not touch upon (being areas very close to my heart they would probably require another book to be written). What I would want to tell you is that Magnon started with two people and two hired computers. In a short span of four years, the company has now built a team of over twenty professionals and a state-of-the-art software development center in the national capital region. The company has worked with over four hundred clients across six countries and has now created a market presence for itself. I am by no means trying to say that the company has achieved what it had to. No. We are still infants in the process of trying to be number one in our focused business area and building a reputed and credible brand. What I am trying to say is that the growth seen by the company has been encouraging taking into the view the very basic resources it started out with. Moreover, the effort, hard work, common sense, learning attitude and team spirit put in by each member of the Magnon family would form a case study in itself.

It was this very fortunate experience of founding and building this company that encouraged me to write this book. This book is primarily aimed towards all those students and working executives who nurture a secret dream of creating their own ventures and guiding them towards building successful enterprises.

But can a book really teach someone to become a successful entrepreneur? No it can't. So the purpose of this book is not to offer a secret mantra towards success and riches. It is just a step-by-step narration of how professionals with no (or minimal) financial backing, business background or cutting edge technology, but with lots of fire in their bellies can build and promote their own ventures. The book aims to provide a serious, systematic and realistic approach towards launching an entrepreneurial project in the Indian conditions. None of the suggestions or guidelines in the book is comprehensive to the extent of universal applicability, but is certain to offer a pragmatic overview of the topics dealt with.

This book will also make interesting reading for those who may not be looking at their own ventures but would like to get into the world of a high-risk, high return curve. What runs in an entrepreneurs mind? What drives him? How he manages and retains his people in a fiercely competitive environment and what marketing strategies he uses to penetrate into mostly an already well-packed business space? Moreover, it may also assist in giving an insight into running businesses on extremely low overheads and resource constraints. The language has been deliberately kept simple and jargon-free so as to allow the book to be a ready reference for anyone who may be interested in the topic, irrespective of his or her technical and business knowledge.

I sincerely hope this book proves to be a handy tool for India's prospective entrepreneurs and even if it encourages the creation of one new venture, I would consider my task fulfilled.

❊ ❊ ❊ ❊ ❊ ❊ ❊ ❊ ❊ ❊ ❊ ❊ ❊ ❊ ❊

Entrepreneurship in India

Welcome to the Jungle

The simple fact that you picked up this book to read is an indication enough of your interest in this topic. One of the strongest stimuli that encouraged me to write this book were the scores of common people like you and me I met during my professional career, who displayed tremendous enthusiasm and inclination towards starting their own businesses. They somehow never really took the plunge. Among other reasons, the main factors holding them back were complete lack of entrepreneurial insight and a view that businesses are meant for people with an uncanny appetite for risk. I'm here to break the myth. I'm here to tell you that you can be a business leader too. I'm here to tell you that doing business is not like gambling. Dhirubhai Hirachand Ambani was not gambling when he started a company with a few thousands in his pocket. He was starting a journey towards a dream called Reliance.

It has been understood and accepted by researchers and industry experts worldwide that one of the most important drivers of economic growth in a nation is the creation of a powerful entrepreneurial sector. It is this segment of the industry that engineers a dramatic shift in business patterns and fundamentals. Conservative approach of business gives way to 'high-risk-high-return' models. Family owned businesses give way to professionally managed corporations and industrious individuals convert corporate ambitions to entrepreneurial dreams-and this entire transformation propels the economy towards a high growth path.

India today has assumed the role of an Information Technology powerhouse and this is being rapidly recognized the world over. Some of the leading names in the arena of start-up success stories have been Indians - Sabeer Bhatia obviously topping the sensation list. At this juncture, I would like to take you down memory lane and run you quickly through what would easily be called the greatest economic massacre of all times - the 'dot com' explosion. This discussion would find its relevance in the direct impact the dot com wave made on the entrepreneurial scenario across the world and in India, and the trail that it left behind in the form of individuals who had tasted glory once, and had the undying drive to succeed the next time. Also, it would give the reader a good insight into the rise and fall of a powerful business concept and an opportunity to clearly understand the presence or absence of certain business fundamentals crucial to any commercial activity. This point would become clearer as we proceed further in this chapter.

The dot com industry started long back with numerous ventures and Internet based initiatives coming up, but the glamour was brought to this new virtual world by a man called Jeff Bezos. Amazon.com hit high valuations and this kick-started a worldwide tornado, something that seemed unstoppable at that stage. Venture after venture sprang up and the dot com fortress went stronger - not with bricks, not with clicks, but with just astronomical wealth creation on projection sheets. Venture capital funds swung open the doors of their vaults to pour money into the new-world economy. Domain names' registration increased manifold and Internet pages skyrocketed. A domain name called business.com was bought at hundreds of thousands of dollars and cyber squatting was obviously not far behind. Technology companies found a whole new market of big buck buyers and suddenly the world was recognizing the strongest symbol of the new-world order - Nasdaq. Literature was being written on dot coms and almost every other b-school student dreamt of hitting it big with her/his unique net idea. Valuations soared at unprecedented levels and the dot com world became the darling of the media. Business magazines and journals looked like fairy tales of successful entrepreneurs who had changed the rules of the game. The glitterati grew with more names like eBay.com and Priceline.com and Jeff Bezos was declared Time magazine 'Man of the Year'. The dot com wave seemed unstoppable!

Heroes' tales travel far. Soon the fever was caught on by the rest of the world, India being one of the major participants. Dot com valuations which were unheard of earlier gradually became common parlance and the new quick success mantra was adopted by many. B-school graduates opted for entrepreneurial ventures, and bankers and consultants quit settled jobs for the greener pastures of the Internet world. Numerous big companies in consulting and investment banking started losing their best people to the dot com bands. New ventures mushroomed on B-School campuses and it was almost unfashionable not to be associated with any Internet venture. Corporations and organizations weren't too far behind. Venture funds offered finance to every 'promising' Internet venture and McKinsey launched 'India Venture 2000'. Caltiger.com, egurucool.com, Ticklewit.com, brainvisa.com, Indiaisonline.com, mba-world.com, Indiainfo.com, Indiainfoline.com, rediff.com, sharekhan.com...the fliers certainly were high. The media again was very enthusiastic about the developments. Dot com companies were given extensive coverage and the entrepreneurs were praised. Needless to say, the valuations were designed slightly away from the basic principles of corporate finance, but then, did that really matter during the euphoria? Acquisitions were carried out at unprecedented rates and figures, only to add to the soaring market sentiment. At the very peak of the enthusiasm NIIT did its bit to support entrepreneurial talent and launched 'E-Mahamillionnaire' on campuses. Internet Service Providers (ISPs) too appeared on the scene and offered the basic infrastructure support required to run the show. Another huge opportunity was spotted in the area of B2B models and this added further strength to the dot com industry. Early 'success' of B2B ventures worldwide brought cheers in the industrial circles. Whatever little doubts about B2C were being raised, found answers in B2B.

Best of talent from the industry, tremendous media hype, millions of dollars, venture capital firms pumping money, both B2B and B2C business models, sky high valuations, acquisitions, infrastructure build up, international support and Mumbai wrapped with dot com hoardings. The scene was complete.

The crumbling was gradual at first and then took the form of a never-ending disaster. The venture funds that had invested millions of dollars on the dot coms, now needed some return on their investment. Slowly, everyone was looking at the earning ability of the dot com companies and the quest for revenue began. Venture after venture, the dot com companies started exposing their inability for revenue generation. This was not only the Indian case, but was also being observed carefully by analysts in the US economy. As was inevitable, magazines and journals were now carrying doubts being raised about the profitability of dot com companies. The balance sheets of dot coms were showing sinking patterns and the stock market was soon the next playground of the downfall.

The first to reel under were the B2C business model companies. Most of them had revenue models which were either e-tailing or completely advertisement based. Moreover, with almost no domain expertise of a large number of players and the total absence of multiple revenue streams, the companies were destined to fail. Pre-set notions of the Internet user base were taking time to change - time that the dot com companies did not have. The Internet user was still skeptical about the issue of secure transactions on the net (especially the Indian user) and the 'touch and feel' factor was in any case missing. To top it all, a large number of these e-commerce companies did not have the required physical world logistical support. Most dot com companies in India too were facing the crunch. Be it yatraindia.com, indiaisonline.com or mba-world.com - all were struggling to keep afloat till profits came in. Business analysts had begun dot com busting in a big way and it was again fashionable to be able to question the basic models behind dot coms. The biggest blow to the B2C industry came with the newspapers and magazines reporting a serious downswing for Raj Koneru and his

Indiainfo.com. The dot com industry in India too came to a sudden jolt and thereafter the decline was much more rapid. The Managing Director of one of India's largest networking companies declared B2C dead in India and India Today came out with a cover story called 'Doubt coms'. Depressed valuations now crashed and the entire corporate sector recognized the flawed business models of the dot coms. Even the dot com companies which were looking strong, for example egurucool.com, were not really in a profit generation mode and were barely managing to keep going and building their brands.

The focus shifted to B2B. A large number of promising B2B models were coming up and this was a ray of hope. Although B2B has not been ruled out, the question was loud and clear - is it really possible to bring small businesses on line and manage supply and distribution chains on the net? The challenges were quickly understood and the long-term nature of B2B business was recognized. The cost benefit analyses, although looked fruitful in the long run, had no immediate positives for most ventures. B2B was a long term, high investment and entry barrier business with numerous issues of neutrality and logistics involved. Matters turned worse when Chemdex.com, one of America's biggest B2B ventures, declared closure.

Eventually, the artificial and short-term market euphoria came to a grinding halt and companies, entrepreneurs, investors and venture funds together realized this (see Box). Now the market is sparing only those dot coms which offer true value to customers and lead to revenues and profit as the ultimate goal. It would be wrong to say that the dot com market has seen complete decimation, and is now functioning more like an industry with ground realities in place. Dot com companies like rediff.com are coming up even now in a big way and a large number of neutral and conglomerate based B2B portals like metaljunction.com and petpolymers.com are about to emerge on the scenes. Although retrenchments have been the order of the day with dot com ventures, a substantial workforce is still employed with these dot com companies and they are even now among the biggest buyers of technology.

Box 1. *What exactly went wrong with so many ventures is something that is out of the scope of this book. At this stage what is crucial to understand is that 'dot coms' as such are just a very tiny percentage of a whole new business realm called e-business. During the course of my research for the book, I was surprised to have come across a large number of working executives and B-School students who considered the dot com rush as the beginning and culmination of Internet based business. Clearly, what they failed to understand was that the concept of stand-alone dot com companies was just one of the business models possible on the net. The Internet has a lot more to offer through its unlimited penetration and communication strength. The real opportunity lies for brick and mortar businesses that have the physical world logistics presence and domain expertise. The ability of the World Wide Web to connect every prospective buyer with every seller, every seeker of information with every source, every organization to every individual cannot be surpassed. Business operations that are possible on the Internet can be so only on this particular medium and cannot be replicated in the physical world. We shall see numerous examples of this in the coming chapters. In other words, there lies a whole ocean* *of opportunities in various areas of commerce, education, medicine, finance, technology, governance and so on. All areas of demand and supply, customer relationship building and service, branding, database build up and management, procurement and knowledge management can be profitably addressed by the Internet. And brick and mortar companies are understanding this. Needless to mention, General Electric, IBM, Dell, ICICI, Citibank and Pepsi are all companies which are swiftly adding efficiency to all their businesses by adopting the net in a big and organized way.*

Organizations are changing and so are managers. Although the rules of the game are still the same, the pace and scale of competition are on a sharp rise. Companies are finding it difficult as well as rewarding to switch to the new world of the Internet. All business personalities agree unanimously that the Internet will change business patterns more fundamentally than any other technological development so far. The Gartner Group expects worldwide e-commerce transactions to cross USD 7 Trillion by 2004. Moreover, with issues of connectivity being resolved rapidly and broadband entering India in a big way, the infrastructure bottlenecks of e-business will also be taken care of. Cable Internet can be seen all around and Internet connections are being brought to every home through not just computers but also television. Old Economy icons like Reliance too are stepping into the New World Economy and are investing Rs. 33,000 crore on laying optical fiber backbone across the nation for high-end data transfer, thus bringing the country on the roadmap of world-class technology infrastructure. CRISIL predicts a fourteen fold increase in the Internet user base of India in the coming years and all state governments are drawing out e-governance plans in a big way. Companies like Satyam and HCL are launching Virtual Private Networks and International Data Centers and every big and small company has recognized the need to be on the Internet.

With so much action already in this arena, the future seems unimaginable. The storms of imagination can only be encapsulated by simply repeating Bill Gates' famous statement – "You ain't seen nothin' yet"!

Indian Business Environment for Start-ups, Risks and Returns

What still surprises the corporate community at large is the complete absence of collective business sense during the dot com days. Almost all financial analysts who bust dot com business models today, largely failed to play a similar role then. Consulting firms and banks, whom I lovingly call 'guardians of industry analyses' were themselves the biggest resource pool for the dot com companies. Any industry is at risk to face set backs that are determined by market forces. However, the dot com difference lies in inherent shortcomings which today seem very predictable. These inherent flaws circle mainly around weak revenue models, under-prepared markets and inadequate logistics' backend. Whatever the case may be, it would not only be premature but also unwise to declare the dot coms as a failed business segment. It has been accepted worldwide that all new industries are established on the graves of thousands of start-ups. Start-ups that had drive but not vision. Start-ups that went wrong but did lay a foundation of knowledge and experience for the industry to later benefit from. As is now evident, the same strategic medium of the Internet is now being used by almost all large and small enterprises and the World Wide

Web has become one of the most critical drivers of competitive planning, supply chain management, distribution and logistics, CRM, corporate communication and market outreach. Case studies of companies like CISCO, GE, Juniper and Dell saving millions of dollars conducting business on the Internet are now commonplace. All Indian and Global B-Schools are training their students on e-business and companies are spending huge IT budgets to gear up their organizations to face the New World Order.

Besides the aforementioned developments, the most crucial contribution that the dot com wave made to the Indian business sector was that it gave an unprecedented impetus to a section which much needed it - the Indian first-generation Entrepreneur. The dot comers came from every nook and corner of the industry and even beyond. No company, bank, B-school or software firm was left untouched. The entrepreneurs were everywhere. This is a clear evidence of the entrepreneurial potential of India Inc. whose warriors once invaded Silicon Valley. A country that was producing tons of quality engineers and managers every year needed a knowledge intensive specialized business avenue. After software, it was the World Wide Web - and the power keg uncoiled and exploded! Even though there may be a temporary slump in the dot com arena and market sentiment low, the last two years have given India a whole new breed of young and talented business leaders. Having tasted entrepreneurship once and having smelled sweet success closely, these magnificent men and women will continue pumping in a regular dose of energy that the Indian industry needs so badly. The industry is already witnessing numerous ventures coming back with bigger and quicker revenue structures.

The above discussion should not be taken as a viewpoint pertaining only to the technology markets. The technology case has been taken up since it has been the most recent development in the entrepreneurial arena and has made tremendous impact to the overall scenario. It must be understood that the new 'generation' of entrepreneurs that have risen after the dot com debacle have not restricted themselves to only tech markets. New ventures have been witnessed in the areas of advertising, call centers and IT enabled services, manufacturing and financial services. Specifically, the call center and IT enabled services sector has boomed as one of the sunshine industries of India and is employing more than two lakh people. Success stories are abundant even now with the founder of 'Daksh', an established call center in the National Capital Region, being chosen by Ernst & Young as the 'Entrepreneur of the Year'. iSeva raised $8 Million in its first round of funding (Source: Financial Express, 2000). The same industry has offered new venture opportunities to budding business professionals in the area of training and placement services, with numerous organizations springing up to bridge the yawning gap between the demand and supply of trained human resource to this manpower intensive industry. The entertainment sector is another area of visible entrepreneurial growth with investors and capable young individuals coming together to launch and manage multiplexes, malls and entertainment zones (See Box).

__Box 2.__ 'No Escape' is a mid-sized pub and restaurant in Central Delhi. The restaurant is aimed towards a young audience and is doing tremendous business by being the favorite entertainment spot for hundreds of customers. The Management of No Escape has achieved this by sheer market orientation and outreach, blending powerful business tangibles with an approach towards customer relationship building.

The restaurant was started and is being managed by two young entrepreneurs. It is a perfect model of the synergy between potential investors and driven professionals. The financial support for the venture was offered by investors with faith in the enterprise and business capability of the two promising young men. Today No Escape is a profitable organization, a known brand within its niche market and is planning to expand into other regions of Southern Delhi.

Courtesy: Dheeraj and Sohrab

The above discussion touches upon the opportunities and areas that are witnessing powerful entrepreneurial growth. But how suited are the conditions for your dream venture really? Obviously, no business can be a stand-alone model in an economy packed with linkages and environmental stimuli. The external forces that make an impact are those of economic indicators, competitive scenario, governmental support and overall financial and technological climate.

Anyone who has been following the economic trends of the country even remotely would understand the changing industry scenario. The 'License Raj' is long over and the nineties saw powerful shifts towards global business patterns. Geographical boundaries play a significantly reduced role as hurdles towards international trade and the government is rapidly deregulating many sectors including key areas like power and telecom. Joint ventures and alliances are being struck at an unprecedented pace and foreign investment is pouring in much faster than ever before.

Let us try and take a more micro look at things. I would emphasize that new people and ventures that have brought in dramatic shifts in the traditional methods of conducting commerce have touched almost all areas of business activity. Metropolitan cities and urban centers are booming with an energetic force of management graduates, engineers and tech-nerds who are aware of financial, operations and customer challenges right from the outset. The pastures have never been greener! All of us need to be excited about living during a scenario that is more revolutionary and dynamic than business has seen in the last one thousand years. Not more than a few decades back, most companies took generations to become established business houses. The old economy was a safer, but slower place to be in - years of struggle, lifetime employees, slow market build-up and captive customers. The rules have changed drastically. Microland, Bharti Telecom, Kotak Mahindra and even Microsoft are examples of how individuals with drive, perseverance and powerful business concepts have built empires over comparatively shorter time spans. Achtung! I must emphasize that all the characteristics of the old economy play critical roles even now. The only difference lies in the additional values offered by knowledge workers, intellectual capital, swifter business cycles, impact of technology and rapidly changing market conditions.

The 'People' factor that effects start-up businesses has also seen visible changes. I was surprised to see the outcome of a small survey I conducted on a sample of 200 students from two B-Schools and an engineering college. An astounding 45% of the students I interviewed were not only willing but also eager to work with start-up companies. This is a radical shift from the 'big company, slow growth, less accountability, secure job' syndrome that most of us suffered from when we were in B-school only five years back! This is a small representation of the perception of workforce about young companies. In fact, during the course of my discussion with a few senior corporate managers who quit their 'big company' jobs during 1999-2000 and jumped into the dot com fray, I realized the true reasons behind these brave decisions. A senior executive from one of the biggest computer manufacturing companies of India admitted that although his company offered him quite a packet in compensation, there was no 'action' around the organization that he clearly wanted to be a part of. Another senior manager of a Fortune 500 company told me that he felt like a tiny ball bearing in a huge steel plant. He felt he was so expendable that he quit himself. Narayana Murthy himself was working with a large software corporation before he launched Infosys. The point is clear. Large corporations and small start-up ventures offer completely different bags of goodies to their people. A big company trains people on processes. New ventures encourage people to innovate. Big companies normally pay heavier pay cheques. Start-ups offer infinite opportunities as 'partners in growth'. And most established corporations have unlimited supply of coffee and air conditioning. Start-ups run on adrenalin. And fortunately for India Inc. the supply of talented individuals willing to be on the High Risk - High Return curve of start-ups is increasing. More and more young professionals are entering interview rooms with a will to take the learning path to earning and not vice versa. And start-ups are breeding grounds for these knowledge seekers.

Availability of finance for business is a topic we would deal in extensive detail a little later. However, at this juncture it is important for me to mention the transformation that the Indian economic scene has witnessed in the last few years. Raising financial support for business ventures today is much easier and professional than it used to be not too much time back. This has been made possible by a combined effort by the Government and private players. You will get an insight into various aspects of this topic in Chapter 4.

Economical infrastructure set-up is another opportunity for the growth of new companies. I often wonder how people conducted business without cell phones and e-mail. Anyway, we live in more convenient times when these powerful communication mechanisms exist. We got even luckier when cell phones started costing seven thousand rupees instead of fifty thousand and tariffs came down to 50p from Rs. 16! My idea is not to discuss mobile phone rates here but to convey the cost effectiveness of their use for new businesses. And this holds true for not just cell phones but for almost all generic infrastructure requirements for running a commercial set-up. Internet use is now extremely reasonable, computers cost cheaper, air conditioners no more carry the luxury segment price tag and even real estate rates are not where they used to be - and all these are absolute essentials for business today.

A low interest regime is a boon for the industry, in a purely economic analysis. As per the basic principles of Macroeconomics, low interest rates lead to high consumption markets and higher borrowing by the industry. The Government of India is trying exactly this despite opposition from several segments of the society who also view it as an erosion of small savings benefits. Discussing whether this step will directly affect small businesses or not is beyond the scope of this book. However, initiatives like these are clear indicators of the Government's will to boost the economy and make it the engine of growth for the country. Moreover, it creates an overall positive environment for powerful entrepreneurial developments.

Outreach to global markets has been another clear and present movement towards better and bigger opportunities for the Indian entrepreneur. The entire gamut of IT services, call centers, BPO and other export oriented businesses run on the foundation of strong international linkages. This was obviously not available to the corporate sector during the license raj. Also, the currency and time zone differences combined with powerful technology support have given birth to completely new and revolutionary business models that could not have been thought of till as recently as ten years back. IT enabled services, which is one of the sunshine industries of the Indian economy today, is a direct outcome of this concept.

Naturally, a majority of successful and high volume business start-ups have been in this particular sector.

Finally, **widespread acceptance and commercial use of the Internet** and been a driving force behind surpassing whatever few barriers remained in the way of seamless international commerce. Offering an unprecedented medium of communication, branding, cataloguing, knowledge exchange and real time transactions, the Internet has enabled Indian companies to compete in the International markets without having to create physical presence or set up marketing offices abroad. This has been even more dramatic with the growth of the domestic telecom sector that provides the necessary backbone for e-commerce, along with other opportunities in the convergence space.

The above discussion is not an attempt to analyze the Indian economy and its impact on start-ups. In fact theoretically it becomes extremely difficult to do so without plunging deep into the concepts and statistics of National economics. However, it is apparent that the post 1991 years have been more encouraging and suitable for entrepreneurial growth. Thus the above is a practical look at few of the key developments that have made this possible. I would want you to go through some interesting statistics that support the view of overall entrepreneurial growth and environmental impetus that you have read in the last few pages. The **Global Entrepreneurship Monitor (GEM) India Report 2002** has ranked India number two on an entrepreneurship index out of 37 countries that were a part of the project. With an exceptional entrepreneurial activity rate of 17.9%, India stands second only to Thailand

(18.9%) and above developed countries like USA, UK and Canada. More importantly, the 2002 figure of Total Entrepreneurial Activity is a significant 6.3% jump from the 2001 figures. Although a large number of framework issues still persist, this growth rate outpaces the global average and is a strong indicator of the vibrant start-up conditions in the country. It would be useful for you to take note of the top ten entrepreneurially active sectors the Report highlights -

1. Computer Software - Services
2. Telecommunication Services
3. Pharmaceuticals and Drugs
4. Automotive and Transport Equipment
5. Internet - Related Business
6. Food, Beverage and Tobacco Processing
7. Education Services
8. Banking, Finance and Insurance
9. Biotechnology
10. Consulting and Business Services

Business Risk - The Real Picture

It is now an apt time to discuss what may be the deciding factor on your way towards planning your own venture - your Risk-Appetite. It has already been understood that the market today offers tremendous opportunities and support for launching new businesses. However, it is extremely important for you to understand the risk factors involved in running your own venture before you take the final plunge.

There can obviously be no business that is not dependent on market forces and in turn the risks that come with them. We have all heard of numerous companies that have faced complete decimation even after years of doing successful business. The number of companies shutting down in their first year of operation is even more. All industries and companies are subject to business pressures and Michael Porter describes them under the five heads of substitute products and services, buyer power, supply side pressures, threat of new entrants and the intensity of competition. When you apply this to practical business it becomes even more real. Even within the course of my research for this book, I witnessed numerous public sector undertakings turning almost sick, several dot com companies crashing and scores of event management companies, computer hardware agencies, export oriented units, restaurants and advertising agencies pulling their shutters down. At this stage we would not discuss the reasons and causes for the same (which shall be discussed throughout this book, with suggested solutions and guards) but only try to admit and understand the uncertainties associated to business. It is important for all of us to treat business as a rational and careful career decision and not something that is started out of some temporary stimuli and short-term excitement.

The risk-taking ability of no two individuals can be exactly the same. This is because risk-taking depends on too many factors that may be personal or environmental. Family backgrounds, need for regular incomes, stress-handling ability, mind space issues, levels of ambition, marital responsibilities and many other aspects of an individuals life effect his or her risk appetite. And there is no one who can help you measure yours except yourself. I have seen many cases where people have taken entrepreneurial steps in spite of personal life pressures and also many cases where people most fit for business have refused to do so because of individual preferences.

But why is doing business risky? There can be no clear-cut response to this question except for the fact that businesses are exposed to market conditions and internal dynamics. An organization can be as badly harmed by its internal members or employees as it can be by its competitors. To very simply describe the various 'risk-centers' present in the business framework the following 25 point list may be useful -

1. Risk of choosing an unsuitable business domain
2. Risk of drawing out a faulty business plan
3. Risk of not being able to raise capital and resources to start the business
4. Risk of legal non-compliance due to lack of information
5. Risk of overspending on start-up infrastructure
6. Risk of recruiting the wrong set of people for crucial positions
7. Risk of unexpected gestation periods
8. Risk of not finding customers at all
9. Risk of not being able to manage and execute orders
10. Risk of bad debts and defaulting customers

11. Risk of losing key clients and accounts
12. Risk of losing key employees
13. Risk of stagnation
14. Risk of poor growth management
15. Risk of losing business to powerful competitors
16. Risk of technological obsolescence
17. Risk of sudden unfavorable laws and regulations
18. Risk of poor quality delivery
19. Risk of labor unrest
20. Risk of Management disputes
21. Risk of inability to innovate
22. Risk of failing to learn continuously
23. Risk of disturbed investor relations
24. Risk of natural calamities
25. Risk of litigation

I hope the above list gives ample explanation for the uncertainties in business. Moreover, this is not a comprehensive list and some hidden risks also surround companies depending on the nature of business. Obviously, the best one can do is to evaluate each point carefully and guard against the ones that are controllable right from the outset. But even that does not make any business foolproof. Most of the risks are unpredictable and appear only when your business reaches a certain stage. The risk factor becomes even more serious when you have let go of your full-time employment to start your venture. As a result your regular paycheck stops coming in and you become completely dependent on the cash flows of your start-up company. In a nutshell, entrepreneurial decisions need to be taken with utmost responsibility and planning. Careful analysis of the business space, research, preparation, hard work, patience and common sense reduce the risk substantially and leave you less exposed. Also, the critical ability to manage risk plays a key role and will be discussed later in the book.

***Business Risk* - Phantoms from the past**

There is another important aspect you need to consider when you do a comparative risk analysis between working for another organization and running your own company. The risk consciousness has been transferred to most of us in legacy by our parents and well-wishers. However there is a marked difference in this comparison during their times and now. During the sixty's, seventy's and eighty's, a majority of skilled and semi-skilled manpower was employed with the government. Although these were not very well paying jobs, they certainly were a package full of securities like job safety, pension plans, housing etc. Understandably, business had none of these and was considered almost equivalent to gambling! And the same view has been fed into a large percentage of India's middle-class even today. Lets now take a look at how the scenario has seen a radical transformation and how entrepreneurial ventures are equally powerful career options, if not better.

Lets first discuss the point of professional security. How many of us truly believe that working with big corporations offers any form of job security? There is no doubt that those jobs provide timely paychecks and some companies even participate in other welfare schemes like provident funds, gratuity and medical allowances. But how many weeks pass when we do not hear about grim layoffs in the best of organizations? A high profile foreign bank just closed its retail operations in India causing loss of employment to numerous workers, including senior management. Investment banks, financial institutions, consulting companies, automobile companies, software labs and call centers have all seen painful pink slip campaigns. This phenomenon has occurred not just for domestic business but also for international companies. The downturn of tech markets in the United States of America has forced hundreds of software engineers to come back to India. The April 2003 stock market bloodbath for one of the biggest technology services companies of the country forced it to think about pay cuts for its employees (Source: The Economic Times, April 2003). And who can predict when the Voluntary Retirement Scheme of public sector banks is forced to turn into an 'involuntary' program due to the tremendous overstaffing problems these institutions are facing? The above is not an attempt to blame any of the organizations or sectors for the steps taken by them towards making their companies smarter and slimmer to remain competitive in today's fierce markets. Its an effort to emphasize the presence of uncertainties and risks even in being a part of the biggest of organizations. None of these commercial organizations can be compared to the security that the government has been providing (and still provides) for the last few decades. However, since a vast majority of the educated human resource of the country is now engaged with the private sector, it is only sensible to analyze the associated risks. Obviously, putting entrepreneurial ventures alone in the risk bracket would be a wrong judgment.

The next point to concentrate on is that business is becoming more and more knowledge intensive. In the last decade trading and manufacturing have given way to the growth of high technology and knowledge based businesses. As a direct outcome, the quality (only in terms of educational and professional qualifications!) of people entering the entrepreneurial bandwagon has also improved. We now see more and more of high profile engineers and management graduates stepping into the entrepreneurial arena, bringing with them loads of domain knowledge and experience. And what's more, this generation of talented, young and educated businesspeople is drawing industry-wide respect and admiration. Organizations like Ernst & Young are adding to the support and encouragement with awards like 'Entrepreneur of the Year'. This has a bright implication for aspirants as it cushions the risk of slipping down the career graph in case their start-ups fail to make a mark. And how is that? It is because the corporate sector realizes the enrichment of an individual as a professional during the course of setting up and managing an enterprise. The need for innovative and driven 'intrapreneurs' is being felt by all large corporations which want to break free from bureaucracy and create pockets of energy and talent within their huge corporate machinery. And 'failed' entrepreneurs are the first choice for these positions. The inherent ability of an entrepreneur to accelerate processes, work on shoe string budgets, motivate people and manage multiple activities make him or her a valuable asset for an organization. Clubbed with the fact that most entrepreneurs today are professionally qualified, the availability of career options for them even after failing to build an enterprise should never be a cause of concern. I have personally witnessed a number of cases where financially suffering start-up companies were either acquired by a bigger organization along with its business model, or its promoter was placed in a key capacity. This makes launching a knowledge intensive business almost a win-win situation. If the venture succeeds, there is no looking back. Even if in an unfortunate case it does not, its only a minor hurdle for your career path and definitely not the end.

By now you are probably in a good position to evaluate the risks involved in starting your own commercial organization. Lets now take the brighter perspective. The more positive view. A view of how lives can be transformed if businesses become successful. And they do! Dhirubhai Ambani, Narayana Murthy, Sabeer Bhatia, Subrat Roy, Uday Kotak, Sunil Mittal, Jeff Bezos, Michael Dell, Aditya Vikram Birla, Bill Gates, Shiv Nadar, JRD Tata, Sir Richard Branson, Azim Premji...the list can just go on. And these are only those extraordinary people who have built outstanding and world-class organizations. There are thousands more who may not have really hit the headlines of business magazines, journals and channels but have created powerful enterprises in their respective business areas. How many of us know about the people behind those law firms, advertising agencies, export houses, hotels, manufacturing plants, transport companies, software labs, textile mills, private educational institutions, agro-services, travel agencies and so many more organizations? These are mostly run by entrepreneurs who are exceedingly successful and have hundreds of people and crores of rupees working around them. This reminds me of an interesting scene from a Hollywood movie where the actor looks at his shoes and points out how someone somewhere must be operating in a captive market of shoestring products and making millions doing that!

I am not saying that organizations like those mentioned above can be built over a few weeks. In fact we all must be aware that businesses are built over years of market presence, experience, commitment and intellectual capital. But then again, how many people make it to the level of a CEO within ten years of work? An Army officer takes about 25 to 30 years of service to become a General (and many of them never become one) and civil servants spend a majority of their professional lives in trying to reach the top rungs of national level bureaucracy. And why just them, even Amitabh Bachchan struggled for years before getting his first breakthrough! So the time frame involved in setting up a successful enterprise is only a sign of a lasting foundation being built. And it may not necessarily take a lifetime to build a profitable business. We have all seen examples of meteoric corporate growth, and that is not a very rare phenomenon. To put it very simply, I would quote an interesting conversation I had with a leading builder and real estate developer of the National Capital Region. During a discussion on business growth he said, "If you are looking to become a billion dollar CEO, you would have to wait for a few decades for it to really happen. Even then there is no certainty. However, if houses and cars are any symbols or indicators of success, I don't think any talented businessperson would have to wait beyond 5 years for them to come". It's a very straightforward and 'non-corporate' view, but it is very simple to understand and immensely practical. I bought my first car within the first year of my business.

I was going through a newspaper report that gave a list of average recruitment salaries offered at top B-schools of the country. When I went deeper into the figures I realized that the averages included the dollar and pound salaries which when converted to Indian rupees as per the exchange rate skewed the entire picture. The average Indian salaries were much lower. Moreover, they were 'cost to company' figures and not the actual salary the employees would be able to see reflecting on their bank statements. On further analysis based on very conservative taxation figures I arrived at a dismally low 'take-home' figure as the true average. However painful it may sound, the owner of a store selling audiocassettes probably makes more money. I do not mean to underestimate the professional strength or earning ability of these B-school graduates. I am aware that some of them would be the leaders of India Inc. tomorrow. I am only trying to compare their personal financial figures vis-à-vis their entrepreneurial counterparts. It would be wrong to base a business dream only on monetary calculations, but as Anil Ambani once put it brilliantly - 'money is an excellent by-product'. It's an excellent by-product of an entrepreneurial vision, ethics-based business, shareholder value and a will to build a company spanning corporate generations.

It is a common perception that entrepreneurs are bold and independent people. I do not disagree with this completely. Apart from offering an opportunity to realize dreams and build fortunes, start-up enterprises provide an entrepreneur some other invaluable 'perks'. These include those of functioning independently, taking key decisions, converting a passion into an occupation, choosing and carving his or her own career graph, deciding work hours and last but not the least, working without a 'Boss'! The last 'perk' may sound a little immature at the first glance but when you really take a pragmatic view, it does talk about a work environment full of freedom - freedom that nurtures creativity, innovation and discipline.

I do not think I need to write more about the implications of starting your own business any further. All of us have seen businesses failing and succeeding. All of us have witnessed fortunes and palaces being built. All of us understand the risk and return curve now. My only attempt has been to take you on a journey which gives you an 'insider' view of business and take you away from the awe-filled mystique that hovers around the world of business and start-up efforts. Remember, it is common people like you and me who are inside there and are transforming their lives with every passing day. They are breaking the shackles of 'middle-class'. They are ready to go all the way to achieve what they have always dreamt of. Because they know its no fairy tale - it really happens.

The above discussion would have given you enough food for thought. You can even think of taking a day off from this book and spend more time absorbing what we have analyzed. Once you are through, you can come back for a lot more of this interesting discussion in the coming pages of the book.

The write-up given so far talks mainly about the track Indian entrepreneurship has taken, the existing scenario and the opportunities that exist and beckon talent more today than ever before. It talks about what the risks were in business and how they have seen changing patterns. We have also conducted a practical 'fears' and 'fortunes' analysis. However, is starting a business all about business pastures? Is starting up your own venture only about economic decisions? Or does it also involve socio-cultural issues? Is a business decision purely an individual direction or does it carry with it clear and present impacts on friends and family? What role do these people play and to what extent? These are the aspects we will try and address in the next section.

Tests, Turbulence and Triumph - Social Backdrop

I am sure some of you are thinking as to why we are going to discuss the social environment of businesses with specific reference to start-up organizations. Before I take you further into this topic, let me warn you that it may bring up issues that have been discussed and debated in our homes for years. It may also challenge and bluntly contradict a number of views and opinions that have been drilled into us by our parents, relatives and close friends. This discussion would inch closer to your personal life than just be a management and academic read.

A majority of the readers of this book would probably be from typical middle-class educated Indian families who are now looking towards transforming their lives through the corporate route. If you are from a business-oriented background and are reading this book to enhance your project launch capabilities, this particular section may not find a one hundred per cent connect with you. This is not because you would have any less social strings attached, but simply because your background has ensured that the people who effect your life are already accustomed to the regular cycles of upheavals and triumphs that business brings with it. First-generation entrepreneurs who are most likely the first of their kind in the family experience the real transition. The transition from service/employment to business ownership, transition from regular but low-income streams to unpredictable but extremely high potential cash inflows, transition from a low risk - low return individual to a high risk - high return professional, transition from an employment seeker to an employment provider. And obviously, these dramatic shifts in a person's life can never steer clear of social and family linkages.

Family Beliefs and Personal Aspirations

I read a brilliant book called 'Rich Dad Poor Dad' written by the celebrated author Robert Kiyosaki. In the book the author powerfully describes the difference between how the 'poor' father asks his son to study hard, get a degree and be able to work in a big corporation. On the other hand, the 'rich dad' guides his son so that he can own that corporation one day. This is exactly the difference that truly exists between families with varying career backgrounds. And this makes a serious and long-lasting effect on the occupation choice of further generations. The testing times begin when a young and energetic individual decides to alter the paradigms. Naturally, as all other changes, this change also generates resistance. Some of the reasons for the above have been discussed under the risks section earlier in the chapter. What is crucial to understand is the overall perception that an entrepreneurial step generates around you. Lets study a few of the issues with suggested remedies and responses -

Risks and Uncertainty - First and foremost, the risks and uncertainty involved with business that was extensively covered in the previous section forms the foundation of all the arguments and emotions against launching a venture. Most of the Indian middle-class is used to a routine income that offers a sense of settlement and security. The 'at least I know how much money I will get next month' syndrome prevents thousands of talented young men and women from jumping into the entrepreneurial bandwagon. The idea of an income that comes in bursts and stops petrifies this section of the society, which is tuned to small salary cheques for over maybe three generations. And well-meaning but under-informed parents will obviously expect the fourth generation to follow suit. I will not touch upon any counter arguments at this point since we have already discussed them in the previous section. The only questions I pose to you and hope that you will pose to your parents in turn are that why even after four generations of hard work we are still desperate for a job? Why do we still take bank loans to buy a car or a house? Why is retirement still a challenge? Why are we still forced to call ourselves middle-class? Think about it.

Societal Acceptance - For my own loving Father,

becoming an IAS (Indian Administrative Services) officer is a better career option than running a ten million dollar company. He may be right or completely wrong, but I vehemently differ from this view. What is it that we really want success for? How much money does it really take to lead a comfortable life? Why do we prefer to eat at a plush hotel even when the taste of a smaller restaurant's food may be better? Why do we want a big long car even when we have to drive alone? Why do you wish to wear Nike sneakers when other shoes may also fit your need? Why do women wear diamond jewelry? The reasons point directly to a need on Maslow's hierarchy - social acceptance and appreciation. Indicators of success are measured on a comparative societal scale and not on absolute individual achievements. Without getting into the tempting evaluation on the true meaning of success, I will restrict myself to discussing only a practical, day-to-day understanding of an established and respectable lifestyle. For our parents and elders, the signs of a rewarding life are a good job, cozy apartment, a car, good education for children, respect from relatives and friends and a reasonably good social life. They strongly believe that all the above come with a well-paying job and that's where their thinking horizon ends. In fact the surprising aspect is that most of them understand that running a business organization can be a dramatic high growth path, but somehow they are unwilling to take it.

One of my friend and business associate's father actually declared that he was ashamed his son took to his own venture and the way its going to be perceived is that his son could probably never find a salaried job! Also, he constantly ran his son down during the first one year of hardships he faced in business, rebuking the entire concept of start-up ventures. Even an illiterate farmer understands the time lag between sowing and the harvest season. It has been three years since and his son now runs one of the biggest telecom peripheral equipment companies of Northern India. We cannot expect any young and inexperienced entrepreneur to strike riches without the requisite time and effort infusion into the business space. What all friends, family, colleagues and associates would have to understand and accept is that founding and running a start-up company is a bold and enterprising step that truly offers employment opportunities and constructive contribution to the society. Business Today, April 2003, carried a powerful and appreciative cover page story on the New Entrepreneurial talent budding in the country and B-schools are inviting the entrepreneurs in their alumni list for guest lectures back in their institutes. My own entrepreneur cousin drives a Mercedes Benz and conducts business across half the globe at the young age of 30! He hails from a simple bank officer's family and rumors say that he is now on the verge of marrying a film actress! I am aware that the last detail has no relevance under business text, but I really wanted to drive the societal acceptance point home.

Stress, Hard Work and Family- A lot of caring parents, including my own again, fear the stress and extreme involvement that business brings with it. They have all read stories about corporate pressures leading to hypertension, diabetes, insomnia and various other stress related issues. And being our best and closest well-wishers they will never be ready to trade the riches of the world with your personal well-being. However, in their zeal to protect us like they always have, they forget one of the first lessons about life they themselves taught us - the willingness to devote oneself to the path of duty and glory. Remember they told us - forget everything when you study... push yourself to the hilt in that athletic meet...don't worry about the scorching sun during your social study visits to the nearby village. It is only the very same principles that determine success or failure even in today's times. Let me put it differently. How much effort do you think Isaac Newton put into his work? Thomas Edison was partially deaf. How many extra miles did he have to run? This reminds me of an inspiring lecture I attended a few years back. The speaker was the Country Director of a huge Japanese corporation. He said that a lot of people commented to him that his success as a corporate executive was of no use since he could not devote much time to his wife, children, golf and vacations. To such statements he confidently replied "Its not because I am successful that I don't give time to family and golf. It is because I don't give time to family and golf that I am successful." I am not supporting any view and feel that family responsibilities must be given their due share. However, no reason or cause can ever be potent enough to keep a human being away from his piece of the sky. And we must also keep a fair judgment of all other options available. In my opinion, running a company may have many high-pressure moments, but it also offers numerous stress reduction choices. As an organization head you have many areas of worry - cash flows, sales figures, overall strategic direction, people related issues, accounts and law, investor relations, general administration, bad debts and key clients. On the other hand, salaried occupations carry their own bag of stress beads - sales performance, opinions of seniors and colleagues, organizational politics, appraisals, threat of losing the job, promotions, deadlines, wage hikes, leave allocation, forced schedules and disciplines. So the bundle is equally heavy on both sides. Even in government organizations today the accountability and performance pressures are on a rapid increase. To encapsulate the above discussion I would only like to emphasize that stress levels and performance issues prevail across the professional band. Stress has little to do with any particular occupation or specialization and has almost become an inseparable part of urban life. On the other hand, the track towards a man or woman realizing his or her true potential has always been full of hardships and rough patches, and one has to overcome these to reach the hall of winners. As the old saying goes 'To be a winner, all you need to give is all you have.'

All the above explanation and write-ups are only views that I hold dear and it has been an upfront attempt to put them across clearly. However, I strongly believe that no opinion can be right or wrong in any absolute assessment. I have offered you some 'decision support systems' but the final call has to be a well planned and screened decision from you. Most importantly, risk evaluation has to be an individual approach. For example, I would suggest people who are responsible for a family and the sole earning members, to be extra cautious. Even if the final 'yes' takes scores of sleepless nights full of calculations and excitement, don't worry. Every moment spent towards your dreams is worthy use of the time.

Remember, the decision you take now will decide the course of your whole life!

❋ ❋ ❋ ❋ ❋ ❋ ❋ ❋ ❋ ❋ ❋ ❋ ❋ ❋ ❋ ❋

The Entrepreneurial Warrior

What it really takes to be one

Albert Einstein won the Nobel Prize at the startling age of twenty six. And this was a man who suffered from stammering speech at the age of nine. Sachin Tendulkar, they say, had a tough time passing his high school examinations. He is today an accepted genius in cricketing history. Dhirubhai Ambani was a petrol pump attendant once in life. What would a petrol pump attendant know about the nitty-gritty of shares and debentures? Yet, Dhirubhai virtually built the Bombay Stock Exchange. Bill Gates dropped out of college and Michael Dell earned his first dollar of profit at the age of twelve, later being the youngest individual to lead a company into the Fortune 500 list! This list could go on...but my purpose of taking a glance at the lives of these great men is something that poses a thousand questions in my mind. What is it that makes these men greater than the others? What led them to the path of unstoppable success and fame? What drove them and how much of divine touch did they have in them, if any? I am aware I am not alone in the search for answers to these questions. However, I wanted to open this discussion in the context of what I will be approaching next - what exactly does it take to make a successful business leader?

Let's try and answer the question with a different approach. What does it really take to launch a 'successful' business of your own? A brilliant idea, a good amount of money, an office, some infrastructure, a few employees and a business plan, right? Wrong! Although the aforementioned are undoubtedly necessary aspects of rolling out a business, they are certainly not the only ingredients required. We need to understand that the basic qualities, skill sets and driving force of an entrepreneur cannot be undermined while evaluating the total arsenal required to hit the corporate arena. In fact, I would not for a moment think before saying that it is that one person behind the effort who spearheads the entire organization's drive. By saying this I do not mean to convey that the other

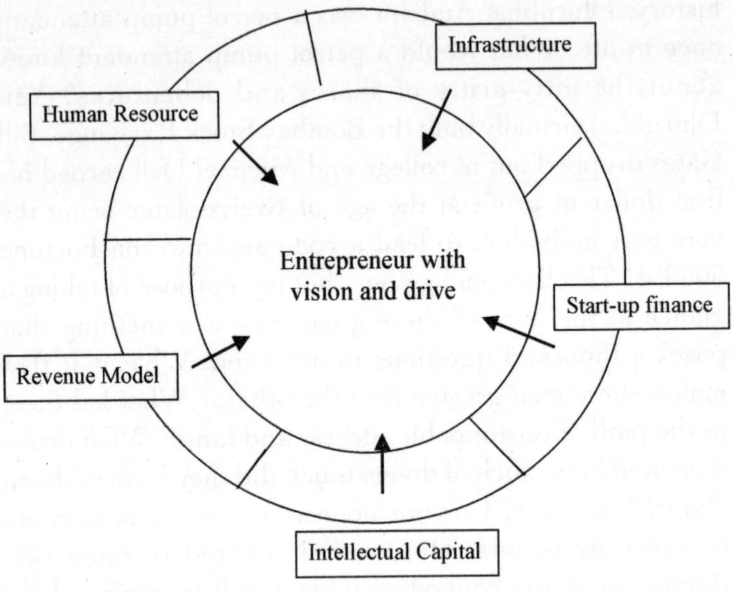

Fig. The diagram provides a clear picture of the view mentioned above. It shows the critical aspects of people, resources, business plan and domain expertise playing a crucial support role to the core of most business success stories – the visionary entrepreneur. The support systems offer fuel and direction to the fierce drive that most visionary entrepreneurs carry within them.

support systems and people play no role at all. They form the indispensable wheels of the system without whom no system would be able to take off smoothly. However, the 'engine of growth' lies in the leadership and business acumen of the man or woman behind the organization. To put it differently, would Ford Motors be what it is today without the vision and leadership of Henry Ford? Could Reliance have been built without Dhirubhai? Simply, would Infosys exist if Narayana Murthy didn't? This aspect would become clearer as and when we proceed further into this book.

At this stage it becomes important for all aspiring entrepreneurs to ask themselves one question - do I have it in me? This question would encapsulate a large number of relevant points to ponder on, including personal and professional areas. It is at this point that I would run you through certain critical personality traits and skill sets that most entrepreneurs possess. This would again not be a comprehensive or universally applicable list, but it will give you a good insight into the characteristics of successful entrepreneurs. At the end of this chapter you will have a reasonably good scale to measure your skills against.

> *Our dreams have to be bigger. Our ambitions higher. Our commitment deeper. And our efforts greater.*
>
> **- Dhirubhai Hirachand Ambani**

Professional Ability

Lets get one little thing clear- no amount of managerial talent, driving force or will to succeed can replace the basic professionalism required in an individual to be able to successfully lead a team and face competitive threat in the world of business. I do not say that this cannot be built up over time. In fact most business leaders have been active and continuous learners in their respective areas of business. What I do intend to emphasize is that this professionalism cannot be substituted. Let us just take a look at the ammunition that goes into professional development and ability.

- **Core business knowledge -** This has attained unprecedented importance in the New Economic Order. Almost every segment of business is becoming knowledge intensive and people have been accepted as the single most important resource of an organization. Information systems now play a key role in determining the success or failure of an organization and intellectual capital is drawing the attention of all business Guru's and the top management of organizations irrespective of their size. In such an environment, will it be possible for an individual to survive without substantial and ever evolving knowledge base about his or her respective business segment? This becomes even more important when you look at the prospect of launching an organization that offers specialized products and services. Can we expect an engineer to venture into the arena of specialized financial services? Or imagine a history student to begin producing high technology microchips? I know these look like extreme examples, but they do succeed in clearly conveying the message. Domain expertise plays an important role in determining the success ratio in start-up organizations in their early days. This was proven in none other than the dot com wave itself. Students and professionals were concentrating more on international models to decide their own ventures rather than following the basic steps of resource assessment - intellectual resource being primary in this.

"*If intellectual capital base is not available to start with, can it not be procured*"? A very valid question no doubt. However, in today's business environment the knowledge workers who may be able to fill the intellectual vacuum would come at a very high price - a price that most start-up companies will not be able to pay. I had the opportunity of meeting the CEO of a big Delhi based software company. He admitted to me that he almost got nervous whenever he had to interview a software engineer. "I was always scared about the figures the guy was going to ask me for," he said. And there lies complete truth in what he said. We all have heard of the astronomical salaries these tech guys drew during the explosive days of the IT market. The same holds true in financial sectors like investment banking and treasury operations. So whereas this human resource may be an asset to the larger companies that employ them, they obviously cannot be afforded by start-ups. Moreover, absence of a solid brand makes it even more difficult to attract highly talented manpower. Clearly, the answer lies in self-sufficiency. Even in that case, no one can be completely equipped to handle all aspects of any business and some talent procurement becomes indispensable.

Apart from the cost factor in sourcing intellectual capital, aspects of project control and management make domain knowledge an absolute imperative for an entrepreneur. Can you imagine an inexperienced young MBA to manage and control the construction of a nine-lane highway from New Delhi to Mumbai? It would take an extraordinary individual to do justice to the project with no prior experience in building and development. So core business knowledge becomes a crucial success factor in the corporate sector today. In the next chapter we will discuss how VCs and investors would come down like hawks on your CV to see your professional and intellectual background. Most start-up companies I have witnessed till today are backed by professionally competent promoters who can carry the responsibility of domain expertise solely on their own shoulders, till their organization can afford to hire better resources.

You need not get demoralized in case the venture you plan to float has nothing to do with your professional experience so far. So far, I said. Which probably means that you now forget the world around you for a few weeks, collect all possible journals, books and website names related to the business under consideration and lock yourself up in your study room. When you come out of that learning mode, you will be a much more informed and enriched individual to carry out your business plans. Also, by the end of the exercise you will gather valuable insights into the domain as a sweet by product. Lastly, it should be hammered well into your mind that you need to be a continuous learner to be able to remain competitive in the corporate battleground.

- *Managerial aptitude* - If you notice the subheading does not say managerial 'education', it says 'aptitude'. And there is a vast difference between the two. The author of 'What They Don't Teach You at Harvard Business School' Mark McCormack is probably the biggest example of this.

He built a huge international corporate group called IMG. He also wrote books on management and street-smart business executives. He himself never attended Harvard Business School. There are thousands of more examples where business maharajas without any formal B-school training created fortunes and empires within their own lifetimes.

So if you are not a management graduate, there is nothing seriously wrong with your prospects of hitting it big in the business world. Whether good managers are born that way or whether they develop these skills over time is still a big mystery. But what is clear is that successful management has little to do with degrees. I am not undermining the importance of a formal MBA certificate; in fact I am sure it enhances overall business view, market understanding, financial aptitude and CV value. However, it can at best be an additional advantage, and not a prerequisite for corporate performance. A substantial chunk of management skill set comprises leadership and people management, which can rarely be taught through textbooks and instructors. Akbar the Great, they say, was one of the most effective people managers ever born. He obviously didn't even hear of a B-school in those times. Almost none of the Military Generals who lead armies into gruesome battles and keep them together have had management training. But the above-mentioned people certainly are the greatest of managers. And business management cannot be too different from warfare. After all most of the concepts of Strategic Management, Operations Research and the Internet find their origins in military practices. So the leadership, people and crisis management skills that a business manager or an entrepreneur needs to possess can be developed, acquired and implemented with or without qualifications. But one thing is certain; absence of this particular quality can largely ensure that your venture never reaches starry heights. There may be professional environments where you do not really need too much of management talent. For example, human resource involved in cutting-edge software development set-ups requires high levels of technology and knowledge capital, but comparatively lesser application of high complexity management practices. But when it comes to managing an organization, management aptitude is tested to its hilt. Irrespective of the area of operations of your company, you will face situations and crises which would storm any organization unless guarded by the strong will and leadership of a capable manager.

What is the true essence of management? What does it really mean? It means commitment. It means leadership. It means motivation. It means financial understanding. It means crises management. It means empathizing with people. It means empowering them. It takes high IQ. It takes even higher EQ. It demands a mission that feeds a powerful and long lasting vision. It means multiple processing capabilities. And most of all, it means a positive attitude. Now if you take a close look at the list given above, you will realize that all its components play a critical role in day-to-day running of a company. More often than not, most successful business people are a striking mix of all those qualities or most of them.

If you are wondering as to how you can evaluate yourself based on the above discussion, and more importantly, how you can inculcate these competences, my only suggestion would be to take the route of quiet observation. Try and spend maximum time with any successful and professional entrepreneur you know and study his or her way of working closely. You will figure out a lot of sense in every phone call they receive, every decision they take, the way they treat their clients, partners, employees and friends, their financial acumen and most of all, their infectious involvement in their work. Having done that, undertake a careful evaluation of their strengths and weaknesses and make a sincere endeavor to screen in the former into your own way of working and thinking.

- *Market orientation* - Have you heard someone talking about a colleague and saying that the latter is a 'born salesman'? What that person probably means is that his or her colleague has a clear insight into customers' preferences and a grip on the market's pulse. That is exactly what most entrepreneurs have or should have. A large number of wannabe entrepreneurs I have met are almost obsessed with their product or idea. Even a short discussion with them betrays that they are so neck-deep in appreciating their product or service that a small hint suggesting a little market-driven change can make them angry and aggressive. Now that can be a shortcoming since a product-centric approach makes managers less flexible and myopic about market adaptation. We must remember that business is more about making profits than making products. And only customer-focused products and services can lead to desired profit figures.

So the answer lies in building an attitude and in turn

an organization that is completely propelled by market opportunities and demands. Start-up organizations, especially, can never hope to spend volumes of money in trying to alter consumer preferences and behavior in favor of the products or services being produced by them. Maybe Kellogg's can keep pumping in promotional resources till they transform the breakfast habits of Indians. But even that would take a decade and McDonalds had to 'Indianize' the taste of its burger to suit the Indian palate. As a learning - not what you produce but what you are able to sell makes your organization profitable. Now add to this the inherent flexibility that start-up companies have. Due to small sizes, vibrant attitudes and an instinct to survive, new ventures are able to mould themselves into evolving revenue models with comparative ease. And this is what an entrepreneur has to inject into himself/herself and into the organization. The best way would be to start with your idea as a soft launch. Observe market response for a couple of quarters and then analyze that response to whet your product or service offering further. Even if complete reengineering is demanded, don't be disheartened. It's going to be another step closer to your goals. A word of caution - do not get confused over the thin line of difference between slow market build-up and negative customer response. You will have to use your judgment to decide whether it is slow acceptance or rejection. The former should help you surge ahead in reaching out to more customers and bigger markets. The latter should make you think about alternative strategies or alternate offerings altogether.

Box 3. ***I know the owner of a leading restaurant in the western part of New Delhi. That gentleman initially launched the restaurant as a bar and pub with a live band, discotheque lighting, powerful sound systems and a classy and alive bar. However, due to insufficient market research preceding the launch of the restaurant, this theme for the outlet was a crushing failure. The localities around that restaurant comprised conservative families and there were few takers for up-market pub joints. The concept of a 'drinking' spot for youngsters did not appeal to most of the residents in and around that area. Within two months of the opening, the owner was almost bankrupt.***

At this stage, the owner carefully assessed the taste of people within a 10-kilometer radius of his outlet. He also studied the performance of some leading restaurants in that area and actually visited them to experience the ambience and themes. In a quick transformation following this diligence, he reengineered his restaurant into a family outing spot and converted the live band into a soft 'Ghazal' group. The screechy lights gave way to soft and hidden lighting and the liquor counter was converted to a fresh salad bar. This reincarnation worked. The restaurant now caters to a much bigger target group between 12-65 as against a comparatively smaller segment of 18-28 and is one of the most successful and packed outlets in western Delhi. Remember, it is not you who will decide the product and service; it is the customer!

- *Visionary* - What is common between Larry Ellison, Dhirubhai Ambani, Michael Dell, Henry Ford, Jeff Bezos, Bill Gates and JRD Tata? Frankly, not much. Except for the fact that they all are (or were) great visionaries. They all are people who built and led world-class organizations. And almost all of them started their business lives the way you are planning to start.

Who do you call a corporate visionary? A lot of people confuse a visionary with someone who has an insight into future market trends. The latter can just be a good marketing Vice President at best. In my opinion, a real visionary is someone who is able to effectively blend individual achievement, sustainable profitability, employee satisfaction, futuristic outlook, shareholder value, brand equity, modernization, ever-evolving growth and societal responsiveness. I know this sounds difficult, but then we witness a visionary only one among a million men and women. And it is obviously next to impossible for common people like you and me, right? Wrong again! I think the biggest mistake you can ever make is to consider yourself 'common'. While writing this book I hope to make it a global bestseller. I work for my company aiming to make it Microsoft one day. I may or may not succeed, but I strongly feel this is the best approach to be taken.

Being a 'visionary' at your stage would mean that you have a strong grip over what you want to be and what you want to do to be that. I have met a lot of young and bright entrepreneurs who are quite effective in their regular and routine work, but have no 'what next?' undercurrent driving them at all times. They probably feel that business growth will automatically guide them towards bigger and better goals. This might be partially true, but any serious organizational success has to be planned for with a clear direction and focused effort. If you are starting a computer networking company on a humble scale, you need to have your eyes set on what that company would and should be twenty years later. You may say that you want your organization to be the number one hardware solutions company in the Asia Pacific Region. Even having a ridiculous vision statement that drives you is better than having no statement at all.

Interpersonal Strengths

Rockefeller once said, "I would pay for the ability to deal with people more than I would pay for any other ...". And once you actively enter business life you will understand the true essence of this statement. When someone asks me what is my responsibility as the CEO of my company, I immediately reply "To keep people happy". This may seem like a very shallow definition of work, but it involves continuous and stressful concentration and effort. The 'people' I mention include clients, prospects, associates, investors, employees, vendors, bankers, consultants and many more. And after an honest evaluation of my total productivity hours, I realized that more than half of them go into this job of managing somebody or the other at all times. Not a month passes without having to build upon investor relations. Not a week passes when an employee does not express dissatisfaction with something or someone. Not a day passes when I don't hear a screaming customer and not an hour passes where I don't have to meet anyone new.

On further assessment of this issue and discussions with other organizational heads, I was thoroughly convinced that managing interpersonal relations is the single most important responsibility that an entrepreneur carries on his or her shoulders. This may also hold true for business managers in general. Moreover, internal customers or employees demand maximum time and energy. The situation is like of a cricket team captain. He has attack bowlers, strike batsmen, key fielders and all-rounders. It is his responsibility to convert this set of talents into an effective sporting outfit. Similarly, in your organization you will have sales personnel, operations staff, accountants, customer service executives and support staff. You need to bring them together and act like a catalyst towards collective contribution and growth.

Let us now examine what the key components of powerful interpersonal skills are. However, before we get deeper into this discussion, I must mention that this topic is very vast and has innumerable finer aspects that go beyond the scope of this book. I will address only two of the most critical and encompassing ingredients.

- *Leadership* - What kind of a man would it take to motivate a whole army of men to leave their families behind and fight bloody wars across half the globe for over a decade? And all this only to fulfill the dreams of a conquering Prince? It would take somebody like Alexander the Great. So the question is, what was Alexander? Was he a great manager? Or was he simply a leader of men? In my opinion, he was the latter. A great manager can prove to be a very effective General during a battle. He will probably utilize all the resources of his side optimally, analyze competitive threat correctly and even win. But can he convert millions of people of a whole country into a combat unit for only his own expansionist plans? No. A leader can!

I do not want to raise the debate on leadership and management all over again. In fact I honestly believe that both these qualities cannot be mutually exclusive and have large overlaps with each other. However, I am also convinced that leadership needs that wee bit more spark than management. Even in History we have seen numerous examples of this - whether it was the Mogul ruler Babur who victoriously fought an army several fold bigger than his own or Napoleon who did that very often, and both only by the undying, fearless and to some extent illogical support from their men. Maybe because leaders don't operate on logic. They are driven by conviction.

From the Moguls lets now talk about the business maharajas of today. What would you call some one like Ratan Tata? After having spent hours with a few top corporate executives from the Tata Group, I realized that Ratan Tata was not just a corporate head for them. He is an icon and the carrier of a legacy of faith and trust over generations. He is probably not only responsible for the profitability of the Group, he is also embossed on most hearts of the Tata workforce. Here we can safely say, he is not just managing the Tata Group - he is leading it.

What can be the implications of leadership ability for entrepreneurs? Let me give you an example. You are running a start-up company with very limited resources, under-paid workforce, almost inhuman working conditions and loads of stress. At this point, you bag a crucial order that will help you remain afloat for easily a few months. However, that order has to be executed within an impossible deadline. Your existing staff is already overworked and is also clear that successful completion of this assignment will make no significant and immediate effect on their compensation or rewards. And the deadline demands continuous and backbreaking effort for days to come. With no resources in your kitty to be able to announce tangible returns to your people and no penalties that you can effectively implement without facing resignations, what would you be able to do in such a situation? If you are a true leader, you will be able to deliver the order a day before the deadline.

How do leaders do it? What do they say to their people at such times? What makes people get committed to them? What do leaders have that is so extraordinary? These are all questions that no one has ever been able to answer satisfactorily. Nor will I be able to. However, I would like to dispute the general belief that leaders are born with this ability. At best, there may be a one per cent divine contribution to this trait. The rest is certainly built up by a human being over years of struggle and commitment. How many people have we heard of who were badly defeated, till they sprang back very late in life? The story of Abraham Lincoln's failures before he finally became the President of America is well known. Undoubtedly one of the greatest leaders mankind has witnessed, if Lincoln was a born leader, what took him so long to prove it? The answer probably lies in the effort Lincoln made throughout his life to finally become the man he was destined to. So what I am trying to emphasize is that leadership, like all other human qualities, can be learnt and developed.

As a start-up entrepreneur, you will face several people related issues during your business life. And as we will study in later sections of this book, your organization will be very dependent on the people who work in it. Maybe your task will be a little easier than motivating people to fight wars, but it will definitely make an impact on the growth curve or even survival of your organization. The reason I gave you the example of the crucial order within a deadline was because you are bound to experience such pressures very often during the first few months or years of work And like the example, you will have no rewards or penalties in your control. It is only the spirit of belongingness and collective fears and fortunes that you have inculcated in your organization that will hold ground in such trying times. Remember, young companies work on weaknesses and not strengths and the only strength you are likely to have is your ability to take people with you. What else will be able to hold back talented men and women who can draw bigger paychecks elsewhere? Also, do you think that the respected companies that have high human resource retention figures do it only because they are the best paymasters? The answer to both these questions lies in work satisfaction, camaraderie, culture and love for the organization. And only a leader can build this temple.

- *People's Person* - I once had an appointment with Padmanabh Sinha, one of the senior members of the famous Egurucool.com. Having reached during lunch hours, I was asked to wait at the reception. Surprisingly, the lady at the reception called the extension of Padmanabh and addressed him as 'Paddy'. It was amusing since the hierarchical gap between them was steep. Later, when I was shown the direction to Padmanabh's office by an office helper, he comfortably came and told me that Paddy was waiting for me. When I met Padmanabh and shook hands for the first time, his opening lines were "Call me Paddy"! This was a huge learning for me. At a time when a lot of companies are breaking down cabins and making open cubicles to allow free flow of communication and kill bureaucracy in the organization, allowing colleagues and even lowest cadre employees to address a simple name casually blew a fresh breeze of comfort and friendship into the entire organization.

Obviously, the office helper or the reception staff could not have chosen to alter the Director's name themselves. They were asked to - by none other than Paddy himself. After careful analysis I realized the depth of this decision. In one constructively planned gesture, Paddy had transformed his organization into a completely friendly and close-knit outfit. What is the lesson? And why was Paddy doing it? The answer lies in being the 'first among equals'. Paddy probably understood clearly that the best way to manage and run a profitable organization was by breaking all barriers between himself and his team. We all have heard of numerous conventional and family owned corporations that still have very evident signs of Management supremacy. This is a strict no-no for new and young companies. And why not, when we are living in a knowledge-driven economy where people are not employees - they are value centers.

This was an intra-organizational story. I also have an interesting example for grasping the extension of the same concept outside your company. I met this very bright young man named Neeraj at a business dinner who was running a small investment consultancy. He and his people were in the business of selling mutual funds, credit cards and other financial instruments. What I noticed about this lad of 23 was the way he was interacting with his clients in that gathering. He had a tremendous self-directed sense of humor that had the audience in splits. One of his clients exclaimed amidst peels of laughter "Neeraj, I don't know why I feel like laughing even at the first sight of you". A lot of the other guests acknowledged the same urge. Within a few minutes, Neeraj had befriended me too, even before I noticed it. Later, when we were having dinner together, I realized Neeraj was actually a very sober and balanced individual. The intelligent conversation he had with me spoke volumes about his true knowledge and personality. Over dessert I admitted to him that I found him to be a very different man when I first met him. The first impression was very pleasant and a serious discussion after that made me truly like him. He very candidly answered that he normally makes a very conscious effort to keep the atmosphere light whenever he is with clients. That ensures that every discussion is within the boundaries of good humor and that clients seldom find an occasion where they could get aggressive. Lastly, the good time clients have with Neeraj, offers him a great opportunity to meet them again and again and thus paves the way towards more business avenues. By the time we bid farewell, Neeraj had bagged my business card and almost sold me some tax-free bonds. I knew then why he was an entrepreneur at all of 23.

Always remember, being professional and serious about your work does not mean becoming stiff, cold and 'business-like' all the time. Ask yourself, whom would you prefer working with - a bright, energetic and lively senior or with somebody who refuses to smile at anything, does not loosen his tie knot even till midnight and wants to push work down your throat? Especially when you are managing a start-up company the work pressure will be skyrocketing. So your people, clients, investors and all other associates should view you as somebody who is a pleasure to work with and have around in general. Participative leadership invariably works better than autocratic leadership.

As a general rule, you will notice that most new-economy entrepreneurs are gregarious, high voltage people who make office as exciting as a soccer ground. They would jump and scream around at work, crack jokes, build colorful offices, dress casually unless situation demands, organize picnics and get-togethers, have infectious energy levels, sit on the floor to get rid of stress and bring a guitar to office on weekends! They would be close friends with most of the team members, they would be the most preferred counselor for personal and professional problems, they would know and remember names of the spouses and children of their teammates, always begin their client calls on a humorous note and are darlings of their investors. They know it is people who make ventures successful - and they work towards it all the time.

Values - do they really play a role?

I met an investment banker who was incessantly praising the Godrej Group as one of the most successful companies in India. This was surprising me since there are numerous other companies which when evaluated on market capitalization, profits or revenue figures, surpass Godrej by far. And although Godrej is in the league of top corporations, a logical list should name a few companies before it. When I asked the Banker as to why he felt that way, he gave me an answer that I will always remember. He simply said that the true evaluation parameters for a 'successful' company are not profit or sales figures - they are shareholder value, business values, employee values, management values, faith, brand equity and respectability. And Godrej ranked very high on all these. I was convinced for good.

I know it may be amusing to see the mention of 'values' in a cutthroat, commercially driven business world. Honestly, I personally feel that you cannot have a one hundred percent commitment to values while running a business. This may be different to what they teach you in your Business Ethics curriculum back in B-school, but you may call it a confession from a struggled entrepreneur. As a simple example, when your clients don't pay you your compensation when you really deserve it, can you afford to pay your vendors just when they deserve it? In spite of your most honest intentions to pay, you will realize that it won't work till you have regular cash flows yourself. In another example, suppose you desperately need a project to keep your company going. You submit quotes for it and so does another competitor. The project would go to the lowest bidder. At this juncture you realize that you can find out the commercial bid of your opponent by paying a mere five hundred rupees to a clerk in the client organization. You can then easily undercut prices and bag the order. You feel it would be wrong to do it but when you think about your bank statement you figure out that your company needs this project to ensure that your dream won't die even before it began. What do you do? You pay five hundred rupees and get the project. So where have all the values gone? Clearly, they have been overshadowed by painful realities of the big bad world.

Does that mean we shut our eyes towards all values and ruthlessly surge ahead with no guiding principles? Absolutely not. Had that been true, companies like the Tata Group, Godrej and Aditya Vikram Birla Group would not be the resounding success stories that they are today. However, like most things in life, your attitude towards values-based business has to be a very balanced approach. In my opinion, a good definition of values in the context of business would be 'to nurture and build an organization on a strong ethical foundation and abiding by a pre-defined value-system that acts as a guiding torch for the people within and outside your organization and has the flexibility to adapt to crisis situations'. You may at this moment think that this is a convenient way to allow unethical practices in the garb of a 'crisis situation', but you will appreciate the importance of the last rider only after having experienced business for some time. At this juncture it becomes essential to discuss a few basic components of work ethics for your start-up company and the code of conduct most successful entrepreneurs follow. First and foremost, most entrepreneurs have very clear guidelines for themselves and their people. How flexible or rigid those guidelines are varies from person to person. But entrepreneurs are seldom in the dark about the values they want their organization to follow. Like wise, you must aim to nurture an environment of ethical business practices. Do not encourage your people to take to unethical ways of working for every small and big hurdle. If you allow them once or indulge in the same yourself, it will slowly creep into your organizational system and completely out of your control. Here is an example. I know someone who runs a plastics business across India. Over few meetings with him I realized that he was almost used to lying to his clients on the status of orders. He always had some genuine sounding excuses that gave him extra time to fulfill or dispatch those consignments. He often involved his sales staff as accomplices in dodging clients and asked them to lie on his behalf. After a few months I visited his office again and found him screaming at some of his staff for misleading some of his blue chip customers who had called in to track their orders. They were the customers he himself never tried to fool around with and discovered that some of his people were doing that on a regular basis. He could not afford that and realized that the culture he created himself had gone beyond his control.

Secondly, most entrepreneurs are fiercely honest with their own employees. I am associated to an educational institution that is run by a dynamic middle-aged individual. He has been able to build a name for that institute within a short span of seven years in a fiercely competitive technical education market. During the time I spent with him I realized that he was a nightmare for his vendors. He just wouldn't pay them on time - not as a compulsion but as a policy. Initially that disturbed me for a while because I was Faculty in that institute and worked hard on giving the students the best I could. Later, to my surprise, the institute paid me and the entire faculty a week in advance. In case we were unable to pick up our paychecks, they would be hand-delivered to our offices or homes. On finally questioning the Director on this differential behavior, he just smiled and said, "you all are family, the vendors are outsiders". The simplicity with which he said this was proof enough of his clear understanding of the demarcation he had to engineer even in his organization's value system. And why not? The people who work with you are partners in success and failure and together form the organizational whole. Being honest with them will bring you back something very valuable - they will be honest with you.

Finally, all entrepreneurs are aware (or should be aware) that culture and values always take the top-down route. You will reap what you will sow. If you have been sacking people without giving them ample notice, soon the others will start quitting without letting you know either. If you have been deducting money for every half-hour that they come late, be prepared to pay them for every extra hour that they work. If you have been cheating clients on their billing, you can be very sure to get inflated reimbursement bills from your staff. If you have been violating copyrights, no one can help you maintain the sanctity of your intellectual property. So remember, a good entrepreneur is someone who has a deep insight into the values he wants his organization to imbibe and the repercussions that follow in failing to do so. Even in a case where some unethical act has to be carried out to get your company out of dire straits, make sure you involve the key members of your organization and communicate the situation.

To end this discussion I will narrate an incident that made a dramatic transformation in my own perception of values vis-à-vis business development. When I was on the verge of completing my MBA, our institute invited an entrepreneur who is one of the people who inspired me to take the entrepreneurial route. He was Mr. Bharat Kapoor, the Promoter of First City and Parenting Magazines. During his spellbinding lecture he told us about an incident when one of his marketing team ladies approached a valuable customer's office for the regular advertisements the latter placed in First City magazine. Shockingly, the client misbehaved with the lady who came back to Bharat Kapoor in a disturbed state. This was a critical decision point for him. On one hand he was responsible for the well-being and security of his staff, and on the other his company desperately needed the revenue from the client's advertisement. Bharat Kapoor not only stopped business with that client at the cost of crores of rupees but also filed a harassment suit against him. Today Bharat Kapoor is one of the most respected entrepreneurs in the National Capital and a brilliant success story. I wonder if this would have happened if he had put values at stake for short-term gains?

That something extra...

Till now I have been talking to you about some very clear and observable traits of successful entrepreneurs. You can understand them easily and also visualize how they must be impacting the growth charts of the start-ups these magnificent people bring forth. However, it is important for me to take you on a quick tour into some very deep-rooted qualities and personal strengths entrepreneurs have which may not be visible at the first glance. When you indulge in a more analytical assessment, you are bound to discover some inherent forces in these men and women that set them apart from the people who work for them. Let us try and take a peep into some of them -

- *Undying drive* - A statement from Dhirubhai Ambani once said, 'I will retire only on the cremation ground'. And he did. What else can you expect from a man none other than Dhirubhai himself? A philosopher told me once that life is not about running after materialistic things in a rat race. An entrepreneur told me that life is about climbing higher till your last breath. Maybe the philosopher was right. But I was personally more moved by the entrepreneur's perception of life's goals. And it is this 'killer instinct' that gives this world people like Dhirubhai, Richard Branson and Bill Gates. Let's now come closer to some less legendary names. I once worked with an engineering graduate who was running a dot com company. His company suffered huge losses within six months of funding and finally shut down by the end of the year. I was witness to the killing stress he went through during the last few days of his organization. By the time the company pulled its shutters down, I was certain that the man had nothing left in him and would probably look for a quiet job somewhere. Three months later he called me and was bubbling with the same energy and excitement that he used to have when he founded his first company. He told me he needed my help as he was planning a 'great' concept and was launching another company. I lost touch with him a few months after that and don't know what happened to his new venture. What I can be sure of is that this man would succeed one day, if he hasn't succeeded already. Not because he was exceptionally talented - but because he was exceptionally driven.

Bouncing back - A senior executive from HCL Infosystems told me that the biggest strength of Shiv Nadar, his senior and the Founder of HCL, was that the man never gave up! Even if you lose a $10 million project, he comes equally energetic, confident and thirsty for more work the next day. Somehow all entrepreneurs, big or small, share this characteristic. This usually proves to be a big enabler of continuous business growth since all businesses are subject to ups and downs and the ability to tirelessly surpass the hurdles makes an entrepreneur different from the others. In fact they say that the true test of an entrepreneur is not when everything is going right - it is when everything is going wrong. Consider this. You lose a big order one day. The next day a premium client takes away his account from you. The third day a customer refuses to pay a big outstanding amount. On the fourth day your best employee resigns. The fifth day brings with it a huge jump in the prices of raw materials you use. On the sixth day you are summoned by the excise duty office for a violation you never realized. On the seventh day you lose another big order. How long can you take it? If your answer is 'forever', you have what it takes to be a business leader.

> **Box 4.** *A very close friend named Amit Kukreja was running a small multi-level marketing company called 'Nirvana' based out of the National Capital Region. He started his company out of very small funds that he had borrowed on interest from the market. Within a short span of time his company was on the verge of closure. Some very big competitors had entered his business segment and his company lost numerous 'leaders' to these companies. I met him during one of these bad days for his venture. He looked tired, stressed and tense...but not out of spirit. On asking him how he will plan his next*

moves, he simply answered, "I will do what I have to. I know people will come with me".

Within two months time I heard about his company from the CEO of another multi level marketing company. Nirvana was being spoken about as one of the most powerfully rising MLM companies in the country. Amit had redefined the MLM concept and had taken it to new heights with professionally managed processes and high-value tie-ups. Amit is now one of the most respected and well-known people in the MLM trade.

The point to be learnt is the undying drive of this young man. He is leading a huge company at the age of 26, is known by thousands of direct marketing professionals and drives a shining long car. He and his company Nirvana Marketing are typical examples of how a thousand mile journey starts with a simple step.

Courtesy - Amit Kukreja and Aman Madan

- Patience - Have you ever heard of the story of two farmers who planted wheat on their small fields together? The village elders asked both to wait at least three months before they cut the crop. One farmer got impatient and cut the crop a week in advance, only to find that he could neither sell nor eat that wheat. The second farmer waited as advised and cut the wheat exactly three months later. He not only had enough for his family but also sold the excess wheat to buy another field. The lesson is glaring. When it comes to running your company, there is really no elevator to growth and riches. You have to take the staircase. And this ability to 'hang in' will be tested several times during your routine work. The persistence and endurance of an entrepreneur is needed everywhere - with customers, investors, authorities, employees and even their families. One of my close friends named Gautam runs an

up-market bookshop in New Delhi. He had invited me for a coffee to his office one day and on reaching there I heard almost screaming sounds from his cabin. Very sure that Gautam was probably rebuking one of his employees, I decided to sit outside for a while. Within five minutes I could make out that the loud voice was not Gautam's. I realized that the situation was just the opposite! One of Gautam's employees was shouting at him at a pitch that could probably be heard across the street. Later when I went into his cabin my first question was as to why Gautam did not just fire that guy? To this he replied that the employee was very critical for the smooth running of the business and he did not want to react till he found a good replacement. Gautam was only 25 years of age and yet taught me one of the most crucial qualities of successful entrepreneurs - patience.

- *The inexplicable* - Antaragni - Finally, I would like to touch upon something that even I find difficult to discuss and explain. It is something that can only be felt and experienced. I call it the inexplicable concept of 'Antaragni' or 'the fire within'. This is something I use to describe a weird spark that entrepreneurs normally carry with them. Why else would a world-class engineering or management graduate working in New York for a huge multinational come back to India and open a lab in a garage earning a pittance? Some people would call such a person mad. I would call him a genius. And trust me, all these attempts made by these wannabes are not driven solely by money, fame or material gains. There is something extra, something more. Did all Alexander Graham Bell ever want was to make money on his phones? I don't think so.

Entrepreneurship takes people beyond just tangible and monetary profits and offers a feverish sense of a mission in them. It is exactly here where I compare true entrepreneurs to the likes of Sachin Tendulkar. Sachin may be one of the richest sportspeople in the world, he may be an advertiser's delight, he may be driving a Ferrari - but above and before all this, he probably just wanted to play fantastic cricket. And I guess this is similar to what Thomas Edison must have ever wanted. He did not want to earn dollars on his electric bulbs. He simply wanted to light up the world.

I sincerely hope that this chapter has given you some insight into the mind and mettle of an entrepreneur. Please do not infer this chapter to be a list of 'essentials' that you need to have to be able to fulfill your entrepreneurial dreams. Not even the greatest of men are likely to possess all of the aforementioned qualities/personality traits. However, there is no end to learning, whether it is professional competence or personal characteristics. So use this chapter not as a scale but as a set of benchmarks. Also, maybe you can refer back to this chapter a few years from now when you are running a ten million dollar company - just to see how far or close you have reached to becoming the man or woman you always wanted to be.

❋ ❋ ❋ ❋ ❋ ❋ ❋ ❋ ❋ ❋ ❋ ❋ ❋ ❋

Transforming Ideas to Implementation

Getting started...

During the early days of my planning a new venture almost every passing hour presented me with a new business possibility. This was an obvious outcome of a dynamic market which was rapidly evolving and throwing new ideas to everyone who was a part of it. Also, it is quite understandable that anyone who has started evaluating the exciting proposition of starting a new business would look at numerous options available to him. I became nostalgic about the good old days of planning a business when one of my MBA students disclosed to me that he was planning to start a business out of three possible areas that he was considering - importing sports cars to India, exporting bananas and beetle leaves or manufacturing cell phone accessories. This made me appreciate the zeal of the individual but it also gave me an idea of the total chaos and lack of focused planning in his mind. Naturally, on probing further I found that he had absolutely no clue on how to take any of the three to a commercial track and whether or not his skill set and knowledge suited the business plans. Thereafter, the approach I suggested to him is what I intend to discuss in this section.

Idea Generation, Research, Feasibility Analysis and Gut Feel

So what is the correct way of selecting a business? It is by far the most important decision in an entrepreneur's life. It not only determines the financial chart for the individuals future but also plays a key role in taking him or her to a path which may or may not offer the professional satisfaction he or she is looking for. This obviously does not mean that the domain decision taken right at the outset is something that you can't change later. George Soros was a tobacco salesman when he started his business life. He later became the richest man in the world heading Quantum Fund - one of the largest investment banks of the planet. How is tobacco related to corporate finance? Clearly, businesses can be changed at a later stage depending on market forces and personal suitability. However, it is not the approach you would want to begin with. Ever thought why most Indian marriages succeed? It is probably because of the intention with which they are started - a lifelong commitment. Similarly, in business when you deliberately burn all your other bridges and get in with a long term intent the chances of your sticking it out when times are tough become higher. And it is this willingness and ability to stay when the others may have left that makes a human being a winner and an entrepreneur a business leader.

> *'A man is a hero not because he is braver than anyone else, but because he is brave for ten minutes longer'*
>
> ***- Ralph Waldo Emerson***

Try and get the perspective right. I am not saying that once you choose a business, get stuck to it no matter how unrewarding that business area becomes or however bright other opportunities may be. No. In fact, it is important for you recognize the advantages of being a flexible entrepreneur running an equally flexible organization. Specially in today's corporate conditions when yesterday's profitable commerce may become obsolete tomorrow and another brilliant opportunity arise the day after. We have all heard of successful organizations diversifying or changing directions to remain competitive. So do not get confused between 'sticking to your guns' with 'getting stuck'. However, it is easy for a human being to misjudge the thin line between 'bad times in business' and 'bad business'. When three quarters at a stretch don't give you even break-even revenues, you would start looking at alternative plans if you did not enter business with a long-term plan. And that is the reason why a lot of new companies shut shop within the first year of operations. The companies and individuals who resist the pressure and keep pressing on are the ones who emerge as tomorrow's established organizations. Dhirubhai Ambani's partner left him in the very formative years of his business and Henry Ford went bankrupt at the age of 45.

Let's now come back to the original question - how do you zero down on the right business? To put it simply, there can be three ways of doing it - a) Market research and environment scanning, b) gut feel and c) a combination of the above. I would strongly recommend the last approach.

Market Research can be a difficult proposition for an entrepreneur who does not have pockets deep enough (and most of you wont!) to hire a professional research company. This leaves you with the option of conducting a small-scale research on your own. This attempt would be an exercise that you would have to conduct single-handedly or maybe with the help of a few friends and associates at best. But by no means can you afford to ignore this activity. In corporate parlance you would call it 'due diligence'. Let's make the discussion practical and clearer with an example.

Suppose you shortlist (see box) a set of three businesses for yourself and put the idea of setting up a retail financial services organization at number one.

> ***Box 5.*** *This 'shortlist' mentioned above is a simple outcome of an individual's idea generation exercise. This may be arrived at through personal preferences, success stories, environmental stimuli, past experience or suggestions. In any case, this list has to be prepared by the individual. This is obviously because you cannot possibly research every business on this planet. This list is an absolute essential and most wannabe entrepreneurs have it prepared in their minds way before they actually start working or researching every possible idea on the list. In a rare case, if you don't have any such idea and you are aggressively looking for one, I would suggest to you what Henry Ford once suggested to all the people in the business community – 'Read a lot, think a lot and work a lot'. Reading business magazines, books and journals for a few weeks or months would give you a basic idea of market opportunities and trends (most dot comes were inspired from the success stories in the newspapers). When you think a lot you would be able to partially assess these opportunities and see if they suit your professional expertise and temperament. Finally, when you work a lot you get a good grip on what you are moving towards and your strengths and weaknesses. Once your initial idea list is prepared, you can come right back into the research and analysis exercise.*

As suggested in this book, you would and should get into planning a self-conducted research. Now what should be the structure of the research and what are the key results that you need to be able to arrive at, at the end of the exercise? Thankfully, if you have the structure ready the results and conclusions would be easy to come by. Always remember, due diligence gives you data about that particular business area and research allows you to convert that data into some fruitful and funneled information.

Finally, an in-depth study and analysis will offer what you need the most - market understanding and domain knowledge.

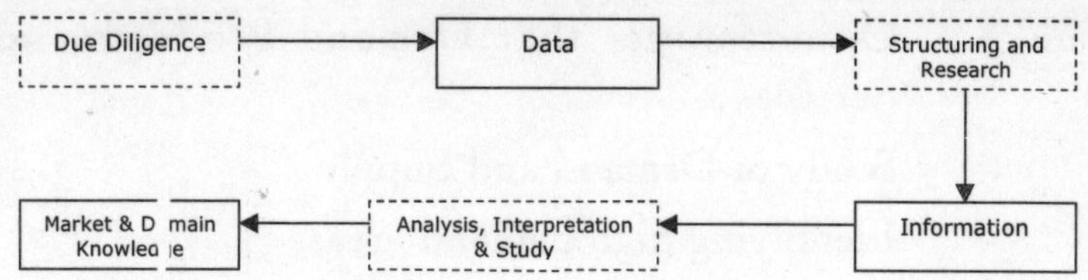

Now lets try and frame a research structure which you will follow to understand and evaluate the opportunities in the retail financial services space -

1. Understanding the Business Dynamics
   - What are retail financial services?
   - What role do banks and other financial institutions play?
   - Organizations' outreach mechanism to the retail customer
   - Overview of the business model

2. Past Trends and Forecast Statistics
   - Past growth rates and market size
   - Current volume of commerce in the retail financial services sector
   - Expected and forecasted market trends

3. The Role Played by Start-up, Small and Medium Enterprises
   - The fit of start-ups and SMEs in the business model
   - Data on business volume handled by SMEs

- Assessment of performance of NBFCs, Direct Sales Agents, Consultancy Services and their respective revenue streams

4. Opportunities that Demand Products and Services
   - Study of Demand and Supply
   - Identifying high demand areas

5. Capital, Infrastructure, Expertise and Alliance Requirements
   - Is it a Knowledge, Technology, People or Capital Intensive Business?
   - What are the key drivers of the business?
   - Do we have or can we gather the prerequisites?

6. Competitive Scenario and Market Conditions
   - Intensity of competition - quality and quantity
   - Who are the leaders and why?
   - Identification of a niche in terms of market segment, products and services or quality

7. Conducting a Personal SWOT with Respect to the Above
   - Personal suitability to the nature of work
   - Availability of finance - self or invested
   - Presence of social or professional network to forge alliances and partnerships
   - Ability to gather technical and human resources

I know what you must be thinking - 'This is so much work!' There are two ways in which I would want to respond to this feeling. One, the list given above is quite exhaustive and one may not follow all the steps and sequences (although each one is strongly recommended). Secondly, if 'so' much work bothers you, rethink if you really want to enter the entrepreneurial battlefield, because this much work is not even a drop of the ocean of hard work coming your way.

Now if you look at the research steps given above and do a quick analysis, you will realize that this framework can be used for any business segment evaluation and not just retail financial services. With minor changes, additions and deletions, the construct can be blended well into any industry model. Point (1) will give you the basic theoretical underpinning and overall understanding of the industry under research. Point (2) will allow you to judge where the industry is placed on the lifecycle curve i.e. whether the industry is at nascent stages, on a high-growth map or at its maturity. This will enable you to understand the longevity and growth your business can expect to have. For example, it may be a good time to launch a BPO organization looking at the encouraging forecasts given by Nasscom and other agencies. On the other hand, it may not be a good idea to try and set up a polythene or CFCs manufacturing unit at this time. The third step takes you into the crucial aspect of understanding and determining the share of SMEs and start-ups in the industry's revenue pie. This is critical, since a lot of industries that show booming prospects are essentially the 'big fish' industries. For example, the telecom sector may be on a growth curve but can you directly plan to take on Reliance, Tata or Bharti? It would illogical unless you investigate opportunities which are present as peripherals e.g. SMS and Internet integration services. The March 2003 Business Today had an article that screams out to software companies to grow up or get out. That may or may not be a correct analysis, but it should encourage you to study the place of the SME sector in whichever business you are evaluating. Interestingly, the example of retail financial services has tremendous scope for SMEs and even one-man companies. This is evident by the growth in the number of channel partners for banks and financial institutions. Point (4) covers the practical methodology for fitting your organization in an industry framework based on the simple 'products and services' premise. The pharmaceutical sector may be on the rise but can you easily think of zeroing down on the exact product or service that you or your prospective organization can fruitfully contribute? You may, but it seems like a difficult proposition. Always remember, it is not always the attractiveness of an industry that determines business success or failure. It is products and services. During the crash of the dot com industry, several models survived and even prospered, Amazon.com and Baazee.com being among them. The reason was that both these companies offered true value to the user that made them almost independent from the negative impact of industry-wide downtrends. It is at step (5) that your entrepreneurial story really begins. It is at this stage where your mental faculty starts evaluations even while you are in the research stage. This is the step where you do a resource requirement analysis and by the end of it you will get a reasonable idea of the things you would need to bundle together to get closer to your objective of launching a successful business.

And this is critical because although you are not doing a detailed project cost and resource allocation study, it still gives you the most fundamental platform to decide if the business space you are researching is really the right direction based on your ability to generate the requisite recipe. Also, a lot of businesses that seem easy from a layman's perception actually come with a lot of resource-strings attached. And it also happens the other way round. For example, I have met a lot of people who believe that medium scale software development requires only office space and ten desktop machines (each worth INR Thirty thousand) as infrastructure. Little do they realize that the advanced software required for each desktop can itself cost up to ten times the cost of the machine. On the other hand, it was surprising for me to find out that a friend set up a hundred member multi-level marketing company in only INR Five Lakh! What is also important to understand at this stage is that 'resources' include a lot more than just money. Domain knowledge, networking and the presence of mentors could be other aspects. For example, no bank will give you a DSA (Direct Sales Agency) status till the time you have a proven track record in marketing of financial services. Or an exception can be made if the Chairman of the bank happens to be your father-in-law. I know it sounds humorous but such things cannot be ignored when it comes to practical business. And your serious Project Launch Management books wont teach you this.

Having thrown some light on this point at this stage, we will push further discussion this topic to a later chapter in this book. The second last step of the research exercise involves an insightful evaluation of the intensity of competition in the market. The example of BPO organizations or software companies can again be fruitfully used here. Software services and BPO are high-opportunity areas, but the presence of a large number of large, medium and small scale players at every level of the business value chain makes them difficult industries to penetrate and operate in. Not only because of the market share fragmentation but also due to the negative push it gives to the margins and profitability of the sector. We are all probably aware that there is little dearth of BPO work coming into India and the real issue now is of the price viability of the jobs. And this is an obvious outcome of the presence of a large number of smaller players who operate on very low overheads and this makes project bidding a tough proposition. There is another aspect of competitive threat that you need to take into consideration. The easier it is to get into a business, the more are the chances of banging into tremendous competition. High-entry-barrier businesses are not always bad. At least not when you have been able to overcome them. Apart from the quantitative analysis of the existing competition, you need to investigate the quality of contenders too. You will have to identify the market leaders and try as best as you can to pinpoint the core reason of there success. It may be difficult because the simple fact that they have been present in the market much longer than you may itself be the reason for superiority. Whatever the case may be, this approach will compel you to gain an insight into the competences of the strongest player in the market and that will certainly be an exercise that leads to serious learning. Finally, after a thorough study of the market space and the competitive jungle, you need to look for the comparatively low hanging apples. The 'Waiters-on-Wheels' case study rings in my mind wherever there is a discussion on identifying opportunities. Some really talented (or researched) entrepreneur identified that the biggest money-spinner in the food and beverages industry could be in bringing customers and restaurants together in a traffic and parking congested city like New Delhi. So he or she decided to make eating-out convenient for Delhiites while giving regular and easy business to restaurateurs. So the decision was to enter the F&B industry via the logistics route instead of setting up yet another eating joint. And the yellow scootered WOW warriors invaded the city!

Finally, the last point will demand extra thinking and logical analysis. It is the last stage of your research and will be responsible for the 'go' or 'no-go'. Under point (5) you studied the financial, knowledge and other resource requirements of the business space. Under the last point you would conduct an inward looking evaluation that will be focused towards assessing whether the specific industry requirements can be fulfilled by the solutions you can present by way of resource deployment. Not only will the capital intensity, networking and intellectual demands of the business play a role but also how fit you personally consider yourself when placed in the thick of the industry. For example, I personally do not see myself enjoying and developing while running a debt-collection services organization, no matter how commercially sound the idea may be. In other words, unlike what most of us believe when we are young and full-blooded entrepreneurs, money is not the only criterion for selecting an occupation that would stay with you till the end of your professional life. Concepts like work satisfaction, intellectual fulfillment and camaraderie are very real and impact lives equally. So think about it carefully. Personally I would love to run an educational institution that teaches English literature. Lets just put this simply - money tops the list of selection parameters, but is closely followed by many intangible yet crucial considerations. Also, do not forget to assess how your network, friends and relatives, can add value to your effort in getting those initial breakthroughs. A word of caution at this juncture - I know most of us would like to be self-made success stories, but there is no harm in using a few ladders towards the heights you need to scale. An issue of India Today magazine described Dhirubhai Ambani as the 'Networker'. What does that convey to you? And no one can doubt that Dhirubhai was certainly a self-made man.

In spite of having written everything I have about the research and analysis underpinning required to launch a business, I also feel responsible to tell you that a lot of world-class organization and corporate moguls were built out of sheer gut-feel rather than any statistical models. I wonder how much managerial study Late Gulshan Kumar might have done before he conquered the audio cassette industry with his cost effective T-Series products. I read in a newspaper article that Mukesh Ambani decided to launch a bio-technology company over an evening dinner with a talented friend! And who can question the business acumen of a man as professionally gifted and competent as the Chairman of Reliance Industries himself? This also reminds me of a line about starting a business that an unknown author once wrote - 'When you want to launch that enterprise that you have been dreaming of, just go ahead and do it. Don't think too much.' Although this goes against all the best practices of starting a business, who knows this may really be the right spirit.

To put this discussion to a conclusion, I would only suggest a balanced approach. Do not jump into anything before testing the waters but don't wait for the rains either. Be sure to conduct a research but also ensure that it is completely result-oriented. Our objective should be to arrive at informed decisions and to get on with business as soon as possible. No research will give you 100% positive indications. There cannot be a perfect and hurdle-free business space. However, you must have the capability and common sense to differentiate between difficulties and insurmountable roadblocks. As the last step, remind yourself that if statistics and research were the final word in making businesses successful, then the Fortune 500 list would be full of market research companies with statisticians as CEOs! Hence, do not undermine the power of research information, but neither should you get bogged down with only figures and pie charts. As the good old saying goes - He who dares wins!

The Business Plan and Revenue Model

In early 1999 I walked into an investors office without a business plan. I was as close to being thrown out as corporate civility would allow. When I was walking outside the conference room, one of the members from the investors team came and put a sympathetic arm around me. With brotherly concern he said "Vineet, before you think of starting a company, lock yourself up in a room for a month and write. Write your business plan. It will not only tangiblize your thoughts, it also makes people like us feel that you are not here for just a conversation. You mean business." I walked out of that office straight into my study and locked myself in for a month.

I have come across very few business managers who realize the true importance of documenting ideas and plans. Even during my consulting assignments with some start-up companies I found that writing a plan report was way down on the priority list for most of the promoters. Worse still, teams or individuals who had no plans of approaching investors did not have the business plan on the 'To-do' table at all. The reasons for this were many. Many entrepreneurs thought that writing a plan was easy and could be done at a 24 hours notice before the venture capital meeting. The other found it was too technical for the want of expertise. Lastly, some of them thought that a plan was always prepared for prospective investors and was not required in case raising investment was not a part of the overall model.

Let us first get a clear picture about the objectives behind preparing a plan. Thereafter we will discuss the areas this document should cover.

A business plan is NOT just an investment-raising tool. No doubt it is of primary importance during any capital gathering exercise, but that is not and should not be the sole objective. Follow the points listed below to understand the merits of a well-written business plan.

- Tangiblizing ideas into achievable goals. If you were seriously planning a venture, you would agree that your mind is in a state of flux. You get new ideas by the hour and numerous thoughts keep mushrooming every now and then. There may also be a time when you get a brilliant brainwave in the middle of the night and the excitement keeps you awake for hours after that. Many of these ideas are so good that you hope you wont forget to implement them later. You would if you don't write them down. Do you recall how you used to prepare important notes in high school? That was done to ensure that you don't forget the critical parts of the study material when you hit the examination patch. The same logic applies here. The first deliverable of the business plan is not to the investor (or the examiner in the high school case). It is for you own use and clarity. A business plan is a reference manual that you and your team would pick up every time there is any ambiguity. The plan will bring you back on track. This application of the plan document will become clearer when we study the components of a standard business plan.
- Chalking out the financial roadmap. How would you determine six months from the launch of your venture whether or not you are achieving the targets and financial milestones that you should have? How would you determine if your costs are under control and your revenue streams are in the right direction, if not in place already? For both the above issues, a clear and well thought out guide

is an absolute essential. And that is the role a business plan will play. At the end of every month or quarter, you should be able to flip back the pages of your plan paper and match it with the actual figures. Obviously your plan was written during the height of your research and with all the hygiene indications under considerations. So it will be the best measuring scale of your performance and will compel you to take corrective measures. Always remember, if you let your business move on an uncontrolled drift, you will soon burn through your entire cash. The example of boo.com is not too far behind. You need to keep a weekly (if not daily!) tab on your cash flow. And the business plan will ensure that you never deviate too far.

A corporate bible for your top management. When you get into the real corporate arena as an organizational head, you will understand the importance of sharing a vision, mission, goals and objectives with the key members of your core team. I have personally faced the issue of bringing my teammates on a common mission platform whenever they wanted to go too fast or too slow on the growth chart. And all business managers would understand the crucial role 'internal selling' of ideas plays before they can be sold to clients and investors. The business plan offers you a focused mission statement that can be used as a ready reckoner every time you need to win the support, agreement and enthusiasm of your own people. The plan will assist you in reinforcing original business objectives and tell your key managers "Remember? This is what we always wanted to do and wanted to be!" I will give you a typical example. We launched Magnon Solutions Pvt. Ltd. as a customized software and web solutions company. There was a time when one of our key clients asked us to install computer hardware in his corporate office. Tempted by the business opportunity my closest and the most able sales manager insisted that we undertake the project. It is at these times when focus versus diversification decisions assume importance. In spite of the expected margins I turned the offer down, much to the disappointment of my most capable corporate account manager. The reasons for declining to service the client for hardware were many. The implementation of a hardware project demands huge investment before money can be released by the client. Secondly, we lacked the expertise in profitably implementing such a task. Thirdly, we were unaware of the standard operating procedures and quality issues of this nature of work. Finally, it just did not gel with the knowledge intensive software company we envisioned right at the outset. We referred this work to one of our hardware partners and unfortunately he is still struggling to get his payment released. It has been six months since. But at the time of refusing to do the project I tried my level best to convince my associate. When my words did not really go all the way into his mind, I asked him to pick up a copy of the business plan.

He was convinced after he read the mission statement. He had contributed to the framing of this statement. You will also come across such moments when you need to bring your team into a huddle and peep in together into the plan that formed the foundation of your enterprise.

- Finally, the investor meeting (s) - Although this point comes last in the list of uses of a business plan, don't mistake it to be the least important. The sequencing of the uses has been done so as to make sure that you carefully absorb the first three points. Lets now jump straight into the heat of the battle - the VC or investor interview. To drive the point better lets just glance through some of the questions VCs will ask -

"Explain the revenue streams of your business idea".

"How stable is the revenue model?"

"Are revenue source multiple or single?"

"What are the professional backgrounds of the promoters?"

"What are the yearly, five yearly and ten yearly cost and revenue projections?"

"What are the market opportunities you are looking to address and what are your products and services going to be?"

Now think about a practical and professional investor appointment. Can you really answer all these insightful questions over a conversation and coffee? Don't even try.

Do you think that the Reliance oil refinery at Jamnagar could have been built without a project report? Do you think a Taj Hotel was possible in Sri Lanka without rock solid research and documentation of plans? Obviously not. So if seasoned corporate houses like Reliance and Tata cannot do without a business plan, how can you? And if your answer is that your company and plans are too small then this would reflect in your tone and the investor will lose interest. Remember, all investors, whether institutional or individual, would look to finance businesses that have the potential of demonstrating explosive growth and skyrocketing ROI's. I will leave the detailed discussion on investor acquisition and management to a later part of the book. To keep it simple, please take a careful look at the advantages of carrying a business plan to a prospective investor -

- A well-written business plan gives your venture a serious and committed look. VCs and investors take little interest in people who walk in for an unplanned conversation.

- A business plan compels you to thoroughly research the business space. And when you finish reading the chapter on VCs and investors, you will be well aware of the importance of deep understanding of your business.

- Investors would not pump in a dollar without a serious due-diligence exercise. Your business plan can be the first and most impressive stopover.

- The business plan would be a warehouse of answers to the questions that VCs will shoot at you. You can effectively ask them to refer to the document for details that cannot be presented across the table.

- The plan paper would speak disk loads about your professional fabric. A 50-page business report is clearly a better indicator of your commitment than a two-sheeter. (See Box). On the other hand, a 200 page long epic would convey lack of focus and organization.

Box 6. *The concept of an 'elevator pitch' is a beautiful description of the need to prepare yourself for rapid-fire sessions. An elevator pitch is an encapsulated monologue of your entire business plan. Only that it needs to be conveyed in two-three minutes within five hundred words. And this is an outcome of the several occasions when a VC, an individual investor or an investment banker will give you only five minutes to describe your model. In figurative terms, the total time he grants is the time the elevator takes to reach his or her seventeenth floor office. And this will happen! So it is a good idea to carefully compress your thoughts into a crisp two-minute launch that is interesting enough to catch the investor's attention. Remember, all investors and bankers are normally busy people. The couple of minutes through which the elevator pitch lasts will decide if you are able to get a couple of patient hours from the investor. And more often than not, the investors are sharp as knives and will be able to appreciate an idea by the way its introduced. So before you pick up the phone and call up for appointments, be sure to have the elevator pitch ready. You might even have to blurt it out over the phone!*

It is now time when we carefully planned the structure of the document. The advantage here is that the construct of the business plan is quite uniform across various business domains. Clearly, the content would vary within the standard heads and sub-heads of the plan.

It is important to note that business plan templates are available like doughnuts over the Internet. I have personally visited over twenty sites that can guide anyone aiming to prepare a plan. There is only one aspect you need to be careful of before you refer to any website or book (including this one!) for your business plan structure. Most VCs go through scores of business plans submitted to them every week. (During the dot com days this number touched hundreds). Therefore, it would be expecting too much that a VC might over look a canned template for a business plan. Any sharp-eyed investor or banker would not take more than a glance to spot a copied structure. And that would be a serious setback to your chances of raising the money. I am not saying that you ignore all forms of guidance for preparing the plan. In fact it is a good idea to go through some suggested structures so that you don't end up making some obvious errors or omitting some crucial heads under the plan. This would be even more important for wannabe entrepreneurs who have not had any formal management education. What you do need to do is to make sure that you do not end up doing a 'copy-paste' from the website or book. It is logical to take cues from suggested constructs and make additions, deletions or modifications as per your own business sense. Also, I personally feel that no plan can be called for a common platform for all businesses. Customization of the business plan architecture picked up from any source would be an absolute essential; based on the nature of the project.

We will now study a similar business plan structure that has been developed so as to offer as simple and generic a platform as possible. However, I emphasize even at the cost of repetition that this framework should be used only as a learning exercise and a source of ideas. When you have finished reading this book and actually prepared your business plan, maybe you can come back to this page and use this structure as a sounding board.

I cannot say with certainty whether writing a business plan is a science or an art. It's a bit of both maybe. What I am certain of is that the best approach towards writing a plan document is to keep it as simple and direct as possible. The idea of a good and professional plan for many of us is a document full of complicated graphs, tables, statistics, flowcharts and sharply fragmented pie-diagrams. But now put yourself in an investor's shoes and picture yourself assessing one business plan every four hours. Would you have the time or the inclination to do an in depth study of tables and charts, specially when you know that ninety nine out of every hundred documents are destined to your office dustbin?! (Hurts, doesn't it?). Cant say how you view it, but I would rather read a crisp and simply written executive summary - and so would most investors. And that is where we will begin our discussion on the plan documents.

The Executive Summary of the plan paper is quite similar to the elevator pitch we discussed a few paragraphs back. The only difference is that it is in a written form. The objectives of the two are identical - to make sure that the essence of your entire plan is highlighted within a few words that convey the commercial opportunity in a way that encourages the reader to go further into the document. I would call it a well-written executive summary if it does not cross a maximum of two printed sheets of paper and yet addresses every crucial aspect of your plan document. Right from the business domain you want to enter to why and how will you be able to succeed? What are the opportunities present in that space and what products and services you intend to offer so as to reap benefits from those opportunities? Finally, a crisp paragraph on the long-term and consistent revenue earning capability of your model is an absolute must. The right approach would be to prepare several drafts and iterations of your executive summary and get them whetted by some qualified and professional friends and associates. In spite of that, it is important that the words and messages that go into the summary are your own. Since you are the originator of the model, only you can accurately express the true opportunity and spirit of the planned venture. We will now try and identify the main headings and sub-headings of a carefully structured business plan. The construct that follows is by no means comprehensive and universally applicable. However, it should be sufficient to give you an insight into the essential components and attributes of a plan document. Please go through the following -

1. Executive Summary

2. The Business Domain
   - Understanding of the market space
   - Market statistics - Size and Growth
   - The clear and present opportunities

3. Your Business Plan
   - The 'fit' between your venture and the industry segment

- Products and Services
- Customer and Market orientation of the products/ services

4. The Revenue Model
   - Sources of revenue - single/multiple
   - Longevity of revenue streams
   - Projections based on corporate finance models
5. The Delivery Methodology
   - Competitive Analysis and Advantage - Why You?
   - Logistics and Operations
   - The Business Cycle
6. Opportunities and Potential for Growth
   - Market share projections and consolidation strategies
   - The growth plan - vertical and horizontal
   - Inherent scalability and competence for growth
7. Costs and Resource Requirements
   - The cost break-up - set-up expenses and working capital
   - Sales and promotional allocations
   - Projections and investment schedule
8. Role of Investor
   - Financial Participation
   - Networking, management and strategic contribution
   - Technological support

9. Appendix

- CVs of promoters
- Copies of strategic alliances/partnerships, if any
- Additional data and statistics

Lets now try and get a chapter-wise understanding of the plan structure. As would be clear form the nomenclature, chapter two discusses the industry segment you want to be present in. For example, to launch an interior-designing consultancy you would probably study and describe the real estate markets with its peripheral segments. You would analyze the increase in the number of corporate offices, retail malls, restaurants and hotels, high income group residential areas and other parts of your target group, within the geographical area you would want to operate in. A fine blend of qualitative and quantitative aspects of the market would be a powerful underpinning for your plan. It is extremely important for you to understand at this stage that all market size and growth figures and statistics must be essentially backed by credible secondary data sources. There can be nothing more unprofessional and embarrassing than to see some critical figures in your industry report being pooh-poohed by an experienced investor or investment banker. These people are champions of industry analysis and magicians with figures. So don't make up statistics. They will catch you. Also, do not spend too much energy in trying to offer a fifty-page industry report. A crisp description of the market dynamics along with a focused eye for the opportunities you wish to address will form a substantial foundation for your plan.

In chapter 3 you would introduce your planned venture. This would offer the plan a systematic structure - narrowing down from industry-wide study to existing opportunities leading to your suggested business solutions. This is an obvious offshoot of the age-old principles of 'demand' and 'supply', 'need' and 'fulfillment'. This will also portray your plan as one that has been well researched and is a calculated conclusion; not something that an excited young individual has suddenly started fancying. It's like identifying and realizing that the gold-rush (industry need) is on and the gold hunters have no shovels to dig with (opportunity). You decide to manufacture and supply shovels (products and services) to hundreds and thousands of gold seekers (customers and revenue). Bingo! You have a sound business plan ready. To be honest, I faced difficulty understanding how business plans actually ran into pages. However, the gold rush example is just an easy way to grasp the concept. Complexity in today's business environment leads to numerous riders with every powerful idea.

> ***Box 7.*** *The gold-rush business plan appears simple. Lest now see how complicated it may get when you need to be ready to face all sorts of tough questions from bankers and investors. First of all, who says there is a gold rush on? Do you have credible proof or is it just a rumor? How many people have you actually seen getting the gold? What was the sample size? What was the ratio between the number of gold diggers and realized conversions? How long will the gold reserves last? How do you say shovels are the best tools to dig gold? Why not automatic drillers? And what if competitors are already planning to manufacture drillers? How many competitors exist? Why will gold hunters buy shovels from you? Do you have expertise in the iron and steel domain? Have you participated in any such exercise*

before? Who will you hire to produce the shovels? Why will they not pick up the shovels and go for gold digging themselves? What will your manufacturing unit do once the rush is over? Will it have the capability to diversify? Why are you asking us for investment? Shovel manufacturing units don't cost that much, why don't you sell your car, wife's jewelry and start yourself? Better still, why don't you sell the first 200 shovels and then come to us? Where will you buy the steel to manufacture the shovels? Where will you store it? How will you transport it? Will you sell it out of one retail outlet or many? If many, do you have knowledge about distribution management? Why do you want to start a business now? What have you been doing so far? And finally, are you willing to give us half of your company?

Does the gold rush plan still sound that simple?

The business 'solutions' I have mentioned obviously come in the form of products and services. You can never say "I want to offer 'something' that will satisfy this particular need of the customer." You must be as specific about the solution as you are about the need. You cannot go to an investor and say that the senior citizens market is a huge small investment segment and that you want to make a financial institution for them. What exactly will this institution do? There are many small investment consultants operating already. So the right approach will be to say that you have specific investment portfolios that are low risk and offer regular and long-term returns. Elucidate the strategic alliances you have struck with leading banks, government bodies and NBFCs to offer the best possible investment solutions. And finally, mention the various value-added services you will offer to your customer that will make you the best choice. Tangible and well thought out products and services are the strongest proof of a committed research and project-planning exercise. Moreover, if you are able to highlight the inherent customer-outreach strengths of these products and services, I will say you are well beyond half the discussion.

Chapter 4 rings the word that is the essence of all commercial activity - revenue! All investors and bankers will appreciate you and pat your back if you tell them that you wish to launch a chain of charity schools for rural ladies. Just that none of them will invest in you. This is not to say that investors and bankers believe in any social cause less than you or I do. In fact most I have met are wonderful human beings, societally responsive and with their feet firm on the ground. However, a Fund hires its people to facilitate corporate growth that in turn comes from profits. It is part of their occupation to take commercially sound decisions and that's what they would do. So be very certain about how your venture would be commercially viable and where and when it will turn profitable. I found it most amusing when two leading businesspeople I knew launched a customized software company. I visited their development center and found it state-of-the-art buzzing with one hundred employees. On asking them on how much work they had already picked up from the market I realized they had none. On a proud guided tour of the center they took me to, one of them said "We are in the investment stage right now. We are not looking at revenues at the moment." "But you must have some ROI schedule in place" I remember exclaiming. They had none. The next I heard about the company was the news of its closure after six months. If I witnessed such a disaster in a comparatively shorter time I have spent with the industry, VCs have witnessed hundreds. And that is what they guard against most - entrepreneurs who feel investment will make their companies big and that will bring them work and profits. Believe me, there is no such rule. Agreed that some gestation period has to be acceptable post-investment, but a strict revenue inflow schedule can never be substituted. All investors are prepared for delayed revenues, but none would support a completely unpredictable revenue model. You need to be clear and realistic about your earnings projections and they need to be based on thorough study of the market, costing analysis and financial models. (A detailed description of these models is beyond the scope of this book. For further study of valuation and ROI concepts like net present value and internal rate of return, you may refer to any standard textbook on corporate finance). Other key factors like the multiplicity of revenue sources and the span of their existence also need to be carefully described. I am not too hopeful if a VC will invest in you if your company plans to service one or too few clients on restricted products/ services offering. (This is the biggest challenge most small and medium sized call centers in India are facing). The depth, width and longevity of your target market will play a crucial role in determining the prospects of your company's long-term profitability. So keep all the following simple in your business plan document - how you will earn revenue, from whom, how much and for how long.

The delivery methodology of your products and services will be decisive in making your venture a success or failure. Remember, a large number of dot com models failed not because of poor management or faulty market plans, but because of logistics issues. It was never easy to trade in mango pulp or diamond jewelry over the Internet. Not because of poor cataloguing or poor payment mechanisms, but due to uphill logistics management. And that is an issue with not just Internet based businesses but also brick and mortar companies. (Remember the steel procured for the shovels?). So if you are proposing to set-up a food-processing unit manufacturing fruit juice, be sure to mention the entire supply chain model in your plan. Its crucial for the investor to know that you understand that starting a company is easy, it's running the unit that is tricky. And it's your ability to manage a business better than others that puts you on a higher qualification platform. This is one of the reasons why previous experience in the domain of business has become almost a pre-requisite with most investors and VCs. The market may be booming, the opportunity may be glaring but 'why you?' is what most investors would want clear answers to. Moreover, it is unlikely that you would be stepping into a business area free of tough competitors. (Unless you have a cutting-edge technology invention or a key patent). So the obvious concern would be as to how you would be able to derive benefits from market opportunities sooner and better than your competitors. Not only for investor comfort, your competitive advantage should be clear in your mind so as to enable you to confidently lay out your implementation plan. Finally, a brief write-up on the expected length and nature of your business cycle would be the most potent proof of your awareness and preparedness to face market realities.

Future of the business and not the present is what

investors are keener on. Also, it is my suggestion that you chalk out a plan that talks clearly about the growth plans and future goals of the organization. A vision statement clubbed with a well-written and well-worded mission should do the trick. This is important not just to raise investment but to act as lighthouses for you and your organization whenever you need a course correction. Moreover, never try and curb the flight of your ambitions as an outcome of the hardships that you face at the time of starting out. You should and you must dream big and let it show in whatever you say, write or do. You will never be able to own a hundred million dollar company with a thousand employees if you don't plan to. It is the same old saying 'aim for the stars, you will at least land on a tree'. But what kind of growth am I talking about? Is it growth of turnover of the company, growth in the total number of employees, growth in the geographical area coverage or growth resulting from diversification? The answer is that it could be any of these, a combination or all of them, as long as the projected path seems rational and implementable. Any plans or projections pertaining to growth and development need to be strongly backed by facts and concrete strategies. You obviously can't hope to explode into a hundred fold bigger organization with a stagnant plan of action. You have to be prepared to evolve with the market and that has to reflect in your business plan. All strategies and foresight into market shares, consolidation periods, increase in scale, expansion of products and services and logically extended diversification plans have to be categorically presented with all the 'how's' and 'why's' explained. You need to display a clear understanding of how you intend to spread wider and deeper into the existing markets and backward and forward linkages that will offer diversification opportunities. You will obviously not be in a position to pinpoint the exact mechanism and process for all the above, but a careful analysis of all possibilities and suggested strategies would be enough to highlight your intent and desire to grow. Finally, don't forget to underpin all this with statistics and projections. By the end of preparing this section, you are bound to feel even better and more bullish about your own business venture.

In the next section, you will push across your wish list in the form of neatly tabulated resource requirements. The investor knows that you are there to raise money that your business needs in its first phase. So be every upfront and clear about the requests you make. All you need to be careful about is that the cost-sheet is justifiable and only a bare-minimum set of demands have been included. (Don't ask for a Honda for the Director, which is you!). Even if you are not a MBA in Finance, you can easily prepare the cost structure yourself. Just use some logic and common sense. (As I have always believed, management text is a lot of common sense presented in a well-framed structure with loads of jargon shot in). Remember to segment your expense plan under three simple heads - a) Capital Expenses, b) Working Capital or recurring expenses and c) A Promotions Budget.

(Note - A number of strategic cost management and management accounting principles can be used to prepare the costing models. However, a simple format has been offered to allow readers without formal finance and accounting education to be able to prepare reasonably acceptable cost models themselves).

Within capital expenses you should cover all the one-time, high-volume expenditures. This can include cost of machinery, computer hardware and software, initial recruitment costs, mobile phones, license fees, miscellaneous infrastructure and even incorporation expenses. Under the working capital head will fall all the costs that you would incur on a regular or monthly basis. (Also, frightfully called 'burn rate'). This will comprise expense heads like real estate rents, electricity and phone bills, bandwidth charges, raw material costs, wage bills, travel expenses and other office/plant maintenance costs. Finally, promotional budgets would address the issue of initial market penetration and the ways and means of doing it. Depending on the nature of business some marketing and advertising budgets would have to be earmarked right from the outset. Some businesses would demand media channels like newspapers, Internet and radio advertising as the promotional tools. (E.g. a chain of retail stores selling branded garments for a target group between 14 - 28, essentially in the socio-economic category A &B). On the other hand, some business areas may not be mass advertising intensive and may require direct marketing efforts. Clear examples would be corporate selling for small and medium sized enterprises. I am not saying that the former requires no direct marketing and the latter can function independent of any mass-media promotions. It is only the difference in intensity of use. With a clear and objective view of all the three expense areas, you would not only stand in good stead at any investor interview, but would also get a systematic over view of your real resource needs presented in understandable figures and charts. This will assist you tremendously in a situation where you have no investment options but yourself. A practical set of requirements listed clearly will allow you to evaluate and decide whether or not you can go it alone. Whatever the case may be, it is a good idea and a powerful asset to have a cost-sheet handy. Whether it is for a razor-sharp investment banker, for your high-net worth uncle who might be ready to fund you, or yourself when nothing else works out.

The last section of the business plan should be focused towards expressing the various roles and responsibilities you expect the investor to deliver. To quote an example of our own company, we once decided to offer equity to a person who was not pumping in financial support nor was intellectually critical. His only strength was his presence in the corporate circles that would have been a gateway into many big client organizations. The reason why I have mentioned the above is to ensure that you understand the numerous advantages that (should) come with an investor. Money, though being primary, should not be the only criterion. Management support, strategic guidance, network build-up, technology enhancement, media presence and forging alliances are some of the key areas of investor participation. In fact a number of entrepreneurs prefer institutional finance to individuals simply due to the belief that institutional investors bring in numerous value-adds along with the money they inject into a venture. Moreover, an inclination towards these additional sweeteners makes an investor feel important towards the overall working and development of the organization and not just be restricted to the function of a bank vault. Whether an investor should remain active or passive is an altogether separate discussion, but a clear advantage of active and participative investors is the loads of experience, knowledge and marketing capabilities they carry. You obviously can't expect to get as much work from the government or the corporate sector as an established institution with years of state and industry liaison behind it can. We will study more about this topic later in the book. At this stage all you need to grasp is the importance of listing out your expectations from an investor clearly and practically in your plan document.

Your business plan report may or may not need an appendix. This would directly depend upon how much extra information you want to push across with the plan. In most cases, a bio-data section of all the key promoters seems to be a good selling point (if the CVs are well loaded). In fact, one of the most seriously screened areas under investor magnifying glasses is that of the promoters' profile. And why shouldn't it be? Imagine yourself once again in the investor's shoes. Now imagine that you have two similar business plans addressing the same market opportunities. The resource requirements are common and projected revenues are identical. Now consider that an individual has submitted one of those plans with no proven track record. He may be impressive in conversation but has no tangible credentials. On the other hand, the second plan has been submitted by a professional from one of the best B-Schools in the world. That individual has ten years of experience in the area of the business proposed in the plans.

Over and above that, he or she is a regular contributor to business magazines and journals. The choice would be obvious for you. In the same way it is obvious for the investor you are approaching. It would be a fallacy to believe that the strength of your business plan would pull you through and your individual professional profile would be of no consideration. If horses could win derbies, jockeys would not be needed. Remember, VCs and Funds invest in people, not in fancy models, tables and pie diagrams.

Other important add-ons to the appendix could be any pre-investment progress that may be significant to your business model. For example, letters of intent from top call centers to out source their agent training to your planned ITES education and research center would be a sound proof of concept and design. Other examples could be alliance documents, with overseas agencies, any government licenses that you may have bagged, franchise certificates from a multinational or an impressive list of Board of Directors and Advisors. Similarly, any piece of statistics that may have made the main sections of the plan cumbersome, but is relevant to the report may find place under the appendix section.

With that we bring to an end the discussions on business plan documentation and preparation. Just the way no business can ever be completely right or completely wrong, a business plan can never be called one hundred per cent correct or totally meaningless. The above-mentioned points are only the suggestions that may assist you in preparing what may be one of the most critical documents of your life. To really get down to the basics of report writing, do not forget to use fine bond paper, high quality printing and binding for the report. You cannot predict at the outset where all your documents may reach, and you don't want a senior vice president from a Singapore based Fund to end up struggling with stapled sheets of paper. Finally, remember that your business plan is a highly confidential paper and should be handed over with utmost care and discretion. The only people to ever get a look at it should be you and your management team, potential investors and maybe some key associates or business partners.

Legal Issues

I read an extremely interesting statement somewhere which said 'If you are serious about doing business, form a private limited company. Anything else is just conversation'. So in this small section I will take you through some of the important aspects that need to be kept in mind to ensure that your business is legally protected and is not unknowingly trespassing the law of the land. This would only be a simplified and generalized discussion and any detailed legal analysis is beyond the scope of this text. The Company Act, 1956 is a mammoth volume in itself and even excerpts that are accurately relevant would cover a hundred pages. So the attempt here is to get you familiarized with some basic law related concepts that every entrepreneur should know and follow. Remember Napster? There is nothing more painful than a well managed venture shutting shop due to unforeseen litigations. More importantly, your own legal safeguards in the company are absolutely essential, especially when you plan to devote your whole professional life to the venture.

Keep the following in mind while preparing to launch your outfit -

a) Please, please spend some money and get a lawyer on your side. I have known a lot of entrepreneurs who plan to get all the legalities in place without the support of a lawyer. If managing these issues were really that simple, attorneys would be out of business. This is critical and you must implement this before you do anything else.

b) Spend some time in researching what form of an organization you should start with - a proprietorship, partnership, private limited company or even a cooperative. All the above have some advantages and disadvantages that any chartered accountant or corporate lawyer will easily explain to you.

c) Try as best as you can to ensure that your business related work is not violating any copyrights or patents or encroaching upon any trademarks or Internet domain names.

d) In case you are raising investment from a high net worth individual, do conduct a verification exercise on the credentials of the investor. This may sound outrageous, but you don't want some underworld money coming into your organization.

e) Finally, if you are planning a private limited company, be careful on all aspects like shareholding, directorship and accounts.

With this we come to an end of the discussion on the implementation aspects of your business idea. I am quite sure that by now your mind is already working towards how you would tackle the biggest hurdle on the way. How you would raise the money without which your entire plan may come crashing. This is exactly the question I wish to address in the next chapter.

❊ ❊ ❊ ❊ ❊ ❊ ❊ ❊ ❊

The First-Generation Entrepreneur's Quest - *Show me the Money!*

I studied a sample of one hundred corporate professionals, students and housewives three months before I commenced the writing of this book. To a question that encouraged them to identify the single most important barrier towards entrepreneurial ventures, 93 ticked paucity of start-up finance as the obvious answer! This was a straight corollary of my own experience with starting a company a few years back. When I floated the idea of launching my own business around to my friends, family and colleagues, I was stormed with numerous comments and suggestions about the viability of the idea. 'You are not from a business family!', 'how would you raise a loan from a bank?', 'why would anyone invest in a novice like you?', 'how long will you survive with your own money?'...and many more angles of the same view. To be honest, all these did prove to be deterrents for quite some time. Moreover, apart from the commercial impact of all these views, the more crucial effect was that of going against all these suggestions coming from years of wisdom gathered by the elders. I was afraid of the 'see we told you!' outcome in case the company or the idea failed to take-off. For days I was absorbed into critically evaluating the thought and there were numerous occasions when everything seemed to tell me 'Forget it!'...everything except a strong will deep inside me that said 'Go on, you can do it!' All this was on my mind when I happened to collide into an article on Sabeer Bhatia. The article outlined the growth of Sabeer

Bhatia as one of the most successful and meteorically risen entrepreneurs of modern times and also that Sabeer knocked on the doors of 19 Venture Capital companies to raise funding for the legendary Hotmail. He succeeded only in the twentieth attempt! This led me to research the whole concept of start-up finance and only mid-way through the research I was convinced that the advise of the elders and friends was not wrong - it was just terribly outdated. Although they were right in their perspective, somewhere on the way they lost contact with business and entrepreneurial trends. The views that they propounded were very pragmatic and well meant, only they were representatives of the 'old economy'. Only till a couple of decades back the financial machinery to support new ventures was altogether different and less result oriented. Venture Capital companies had not arrived on the scene, banks demanded collaterals of promoters against loans (some of them still do!), angel investors were unheard of and only the government set up a few institutions to spur entrepreneurship in the country and even their realized financial support to new ventures was dismal. The scene has changed dramatically. Not only is the government more active in promoting new businesses, but also the private sector that has emerged as a vibrant hatchery for entrepreneurial ventures. This combination of the state support and private players is empowering bright young professionals to enter the corporate playground as business leaders, without essentially being from business families or having financial back-up though inheritance. I am by no means undermining family owned businesses, which in themselves offer enriching examples of entrepreneurial energy and corporate turn-arounds, Kabir Mulchandani being a powerful story. However, businesses passed on in legacy provide relatively stable platforms for corporate growth. In today's economic scenario, business lineage can at most be an advantage and definitely not a prerequisite. As a corollary, ventures are not dependent on self-finance anymore and serious wannabe entrepreneurs can realistically dream of launching and running companies with external investor support. As the old angel investor statement goes 'Let there be entrepreneurs with powerful ideas, market orientation, good CVs and drive. After all these money is a non-issue which goes way down on the priority list.'

At this juncture I will elaborate the entire picture of start-up finance options for you, to enable you to get a good overview of the various sources you can optimally use to get the initial capital for your dream project. This will serve a dual purpose. One, it will highlight the importance and availability of investors for new businesses. And two, it will save you from putting in days of precious time in conducting the same research - days which can be effectively used to chalk out business plans and strategies.

Sources of Investment - A Practical Analysis

We all need to be aware and convinced that money for new businesses is available, and is being picked up from the market and used by the most enterprising. Had this not been true, the entire business life cycle would come to a grinding halt. New businesses are the fountainhead of overall economic development and are not just present but also badly needed. And when they play such a vital role and are emerging rapidly, someone is obviously funding them! The important questions are 'who are the people or organizations that fund start-ups?', 'why do they do it?' and 'how can I reach out to these potential investors?' The above are valid questions which got jammed into my brain circuits when I was groping around for project financing options. And I am quite certain they challenge the minds of all wannabe entrepreneurs equally. It is exactly this set of questions that I would attempt to address in the coming pages.

Start-up Finance - The Investor Spectrum

I would not say that financing options available to new ventures come in bagfuls. However, it would be wrong to assume that they are too few either. There are several alternatives that a budding entrepreneur can target to overcome the first hurdle towards launching a business. Concentrate on the write-ups that follow and don't forget to go through the advantages and disadvantages of each of the options enlisted.

Debt Capital

To put it in very simple words, debt capital entails loans that you may take from banks, financial institutions or from a rich relative or family friend. This is the oldest and most widespread form of funding for new companies. Having said that, I find it essential to state that raising money in this from is a tough proposition. And paying it back is even tougher.

The difficulty I have mentioned above arises from the conservative approach that most established banks, institutions and lenders normally follow. The reason for this is amply clear - defaulting borrowers. If you study Indian economics to some detail, it will be revealed to you that the biggest roadblock towards rural financing by these institutions has been the rate of bad debts and defaulted payments. Although this sounds like a historical perspective of bank finance in India, the roots of lending dynamics can be traced to these grass root level upheavals. Even during the developmental decades of the 60's, 70's and 80's, banks played a pivotal role in project financing. Institutions like SIDBI (Small Industries Development Bank of India) and IDBI were set-up to further give an impetus to this responsibility of the banking sector. Nationalized banks and financial institutions even now form a large section of the industrial lending machinery. However, it becomes vital for us to identify the difference between Project Financing and Venture Funding at this stage. Most Banks and Venture Funds are diametrically opposite in the basic philosophy behind investments or lending. Normally banks are more inclined towards safer investment propositions that rely on secure business fundamentals and tangible models. For example, most likely a bank would be willing to lend to a computer hardware manufacturing unit more than to a biotechnology organization involved in high-technology genome researches. Also, it is crucial to understand that bank financing is easier when it comes to expansion or diversification plans, than new venture funding.

Even today when you look around yourself you will find that although banks and NBFCs are aggressively looking to sell their home loans and credit card services, they still undergo elaborate due diligence and verifications before such deals are finally frozen. Mobile telephony operators indulge in extensive documentation before cellular connections are activated and personal loans' approvals demand proof of repayment capability. The internal policies of these organizations make it apparently clear to their fleet on street and operations level staff - 'Watch out for the defaulter!'

When cellular operators demand security money, credit card companies request for bank statements and personal loan agents ask for copies of income tax returns, and all this for a few thousands or lakhs, imagine the sweat on the forehead of the business loans approving officer when you walk into his office with a business plan that needs a million dollars! (On a humorous note, some such officers have confessed to me that they concentrate more on saving their own jobs than on the ROI analysis in the prospective borrower's presentation). As an outcome of the tremendous responsibility of gainfully getting the money of the lending institution back, the loan sanctioning authorities obviously look for several credibility measurement tools. These can include the applicant's career background, proven strengths of the management team, projected cash flows of the proposed business and finally a decision on what primary securities and collaterals need to be tied up. The risk infusion occurs when these include personal assets of the applicants. Along with the above, there are numerous internal policies and programs which govern the lending decisions of banks. However, some banks have separate vehicles for regular business loans and new venture funding. For example, Canara Bank has a specialized institution called Canbank Venture Capital

Fund Ltd. which has assisted 50 start-ups aggregating to Rs. 39.23 crores till August 2002. The Fund's most recent equity investment was made in Telesis Technologies, an IT Products company, in June 2003. Similarly, the Bank's National Equity Fund (NEF) Scheme can be of tremendous interest to you in case your funding needs do not exceed Rs. 50 lakh. But overall, it is an uphill task to try and identify new venture financing options from banks simply due to a serious shortage in the number of bank financed venture funds and the collaterals that make the bargain painful.

In such a scenario, the best you can do is to approach leading banks that have a track record of start-up lending with a professional business plan and attitude. Even in a case where you are unable to raise money immediately, you might come across a friendly banker who takes keen interest in your plan and promises to back you during your second round of funding.

Advantages of Debt Financing -

1. A large number of institutions fund start-ups in a 65:35 debt equity ratio. This makes borrowing an easier experience.

2. Bank financing comes in the form of Term Loans. This freezes repayment plans and periods right at the outset, allowing the borrower to work out cash flows accordingly and set repayment targets.

Disadvantages of Debt Financing -

1. Interest rates on the loan amount can erode your

profitability unless you stick religiously to the payback terms. This is the single most important barrier towards bank borrowing. Moreover, any slippage in repayment triggers a snowball effect that makes repayments increasingly difficult and gets the borrower into a debt spiral.

2. Starting a business with interest laden borrowed money may prove to be a psychological impediment. Although it is nothing unusual for seasoned businesspeople, it may not be a comfort zone for you as a first-time entrepreneur.

Thus bank loans should be resorted to only when you are certain about your revenue streams. Also, it may be prudent to pick up money in this form when it is being used to finance some tangible assets like real estate, trucks, offices, machinery etc. that can be pledged as primary securities without involving your personal assets. I am not foraying further into this topic simply because of its limited real-world applicability to new businesses. Moreover, I personally propound equity-based participation from investors, which I strongly feel allows the entrepreneur to concentrate solely on business development and other growth related issues and not get bogged down by loan repayment tensions. Finally, if bank borrowing cannot be avoided, make sure it strikes a good balance in your debt-equity ratio analysis. Bank loans can be clubbed with equity participation from high net worth individuals, which we will study a few pages later.

Venture Capital - Down, but not Out!

Did you know from where they say venture capital originates? From Columbus! Columbus raised money to finance his voyage. It was risky, but can anyone ever calculate the return on that investment? The return was what we today call America! This is exactly the principle venture capital companies work on - being part of high risk to share extraordinary profits later. Encouragingly, the concept of venture capital has emerged powerfully in India, especially over the last decade. A large number of US, Singapore and Europe based funds have displayed significant interest in the Indian markets and numerous venture capital institutions have been set up in the country. In fact, a peep down investment lane would witness many start-up organizations that not only raised huge sums of money to fund new ventures, but also hit headlines doing that. Egurucool.com boasted of Chrysalis and Star and several call centers and BPO organizations picked up whopping figures of investment. In 2001, India was ranked as the third most active VC market in Asia-Pacific (excluding Japan). In the same year, Venture funds invested $907.58 million in Indian companies. As per the latest report of the IVCA, there were 57 active venture funds in India in 2001 with an average investment value of each deal at $7.89 million! Also, 19 exits were witnessed during this year. In fact, it was this tremendous support VCs offered which made the dot com industry hit the skies in an unbelievably short span of time. Although the dot com dust has settled, the VCs remain.

To my surprise, I have met numerous very knowledgeable professionals during the last one-year who believe that the VC dream is over for Indian entrepreneurs. Some of them very vehemently commented that the poor portfolio results of VCs have discouraged them from investing into new ventures. These are obviously comments made without any research underpinning. Venture Capital companies may be watchful but their presence cannot be ignored by enterprising entrepreneurs. The number of investments has undoubtedly reduced but promising entrepreneurs and companies are raising money from these Funds even now. Chrys Capital Investments pumped money into Mphasis BFL in 2001, Global Vantedge in 2001 and New Path Ventures, a company focused on semiconductor systems, in the year 2002. Also, in 2002 Chrys Capital invested in Ephinay, a finance and accounting outsourcing company. In 2003, CitiVentures co-invested with CDC and Chrys Cap into a new private sector bank. I have already mentioned the 2003 investment of Canbank VC Fund in Telesis in the previous section. Similarly, there are numerous other funds like WestBridge Capital Partners, Connect Capital, Waygate Capital and CitiVentures who are actively encouraging entrepreneurs. Realistically, you may not find funding from these institutions as widespread and accessible as it used to be till a year back. Also, the VCs are now keener to invest in growth stage companies that need financial support for further development, since these are organizations that have proven their ability to generate revenue and profits (a related topic called 'Proof of Concept' will be discussed later in this chapter). However, there is nothing that should stop you from making a full-blown effort towards pushing the blueprint of your business across as many VC tables as possible. Apart from the valuable learning you will gather interacting with these stalwarts of entrepreneur-evaluation, you may also be able to impress them with the viability of your idea and actually partner them.

A word of caution at this stage - VCs normally invest in only 'high risk, high innovation' businesses (remember Columbus?), which in today's market context may be construed as technology-oriented businesses. In other words, VCs may not be too keen to invest in entrepreneurs who want to set up restaurants or manufacture cables and carpets. A VC would invest a million dollars into a business with a view to earn twenty million a few years later. And seemingly, only technology start-ups offer such exponential growth opportunities. But when I say 'technology' I cover innumerable possibilities in the areas of software, hardware, Internet, telecom, IT enabled services, biotechnology, consulting and more. However, even for VCs exceptions always exist and you can approach them in case you can assure them of high ROIs.

Venture Capital Companies - What is in it for them?

Why do venture capital organizations invest precious money into start-ups, most of which are destined to fail? Because some of them don't fail. And the ones that reach success, payback returns that not only offset the losses caused by failed investments but also bring in huge profits.

Venture Capitalists function on a simple concept (which does not remain that simple when it comes to implementation). They carefully select business plans backed by good ideas, professional teams and driven entrepreneurs. (All these have been covered extensively in later sections). Most VCs invest in a balanced portfolio of start-ups so as to minimize their risk by hedging their bets. So more often than not you would see a VC fund a B2C dot com at one end of the band and a tangible call center facility on the other. This guards them against too much exposure to the risk factors of any one business area. On the other hand it gives them the opportunity to operate in a wide spectrum of the industry that offers high return prospects from more than one investment.

The VC methodology can be understood easily. VCs do not invest into companies with an intention to remain associated for hundred years. They stress on relatively short-term investments with extraordinary return prospects. For this reason VCs always work on structures which allow them smooth and early exit options. To put it very simply for better understanding, VCs would look at pumping in one million dollars for a 25% per cent stake in a start-up, wait for it to reach 20 million USD valuation and then sell-off their 25% equity share for 5 million. This is one of the reasons why the timing and stage of investment becomes crucial for VC funds. Also do not let the 'millions' being mentioned dishearten you if you have a smaller business plan. VCs also invest as low as 50,000 USD (or even ten lakh rupees) at times depending on the scale of funding requirements.

A careful look at the above diagram would help you get a clearer overview of the VC funding concept. The flowchart starts with VC support to four start-up companies. Two of the companies in this portfolio fail to take off despite the investment and lead to losses for the VC organization. One of the four emerges with higher net worth that allows the

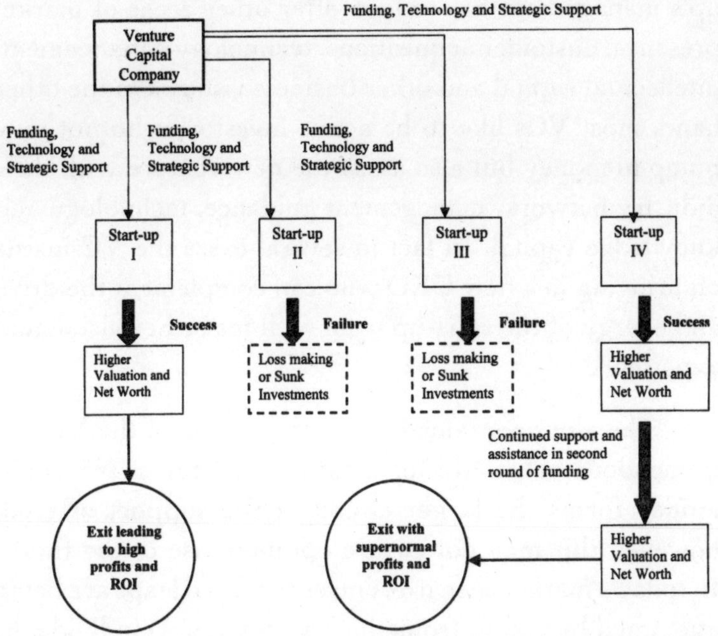

VC fund to make strategic exit with high profits. The fourth case, the start-up again comes on to a high growth track and here the VC stays on and helps the start-up in not only maintaining the growth but also in raising the second round of investment from other institutions. It is that stage that the VC exits with extraordinary returns on the initial investment. Most importantly the returns offered by the sum of the circular boxes are much higher than the losses caused by the dotted boxes.

At this stage it becomes crucial to differentiate between 'passive' and 'active' investors. Passive investors are those VC funds that restrict their participation only to financial support. They inject requisite funds into the start-ups they select and play a 'wait and watch' role. The start-up's management has to look after other areas of market presence, customer acquisitions, technology enhancement, intellectual capital and other business issues. On the other hand, most VCs like to be active investors who not only pump in money but also assist the new venture with their industry network, management guidance, technology and knowledge capital. In fact in several cases the VC insists on bringing in a new CEO who can complement the drive and energy of the start-up team with his or her vision and experience.

The aforementioned 'non-money' role of the VC is a tremendous value-add for most new ventures. No doubt money forms the larger chunk of the support offered, however, this may not ensure optimum use of the funds. In today's market scenario, entrepreneurial leaps are being attempted by young (sometimes very young!) individuals. Although this fraternity beams with undying spirit and creativity, it sometimes lacks the business fundamentals and knowledge required to convert dreams into money-spinners. I know of numerous start-up organizations that have jumped into altogether new realms of business with the help and support of seasoned VC teams. Domain expertise, which may take years to develop, is offered in tried and tested formats to the young companies by the VC funds. Networking is another critical contribution made by funding organizations. A lot of new companies get introduced to well-paying clients by these funds. New ventures that operate on a local geographical scale suddenly reach international markets. In this way, the active VC plays a comprehensive support function. Business plans are whetted, money is pumped in, management is made more market oriented, intellectual capital is handed over and strategic clients are introduced to enable regular revenue streams.

Venture Capital and You!

So venture capital institutions are swarming the place. Ventures are being funded and start-ups are being transformed into big enterprises. However, is it all really that simple? Once you step out to hunt for VC finance, you will discover it is not. In fact somebody who had been trying to raise money through the VC route, beautifully described the scenario using the title of a song 'Heavy cloud but no rain'! What this probably denotes is that the number of VCs in the market and the numerous investments being made by them cannot be a true indicator of the difficulties involved in actually getting them to partner you. It is a straight question of demand and supply. No matter how good the 'supply' of venture capital be in the market, if the demand for investments is much higher the struggle to get a share of the pie can prove to be Herculean. In fact during the peak of the tech markets boom, a technology venture fund would normally get over a hundred business plans and proposals everyday. We can be quite sure that this number would not have gone below a score even now. So the quest is in winning the race among this heap of proposals.

I will now do a VC 'behavior' analysis and try and suggest a few tricks and tactics to be able to draw maximum mileage out of your VC interfaces. However, it is absolutely imperative for you to understand that these techniques can at best be an icing on the cake - the high revenue potential business concept. It is like this. If you are not a good footballer, no amount of world-class sports gear can make you strike that match-winning goal. So treat these suggestions as pure value-adds that will make your business idea look and sound good at the skin-deep level. Eventually it will be the strength of the business model that will see you through.

Take a look at the points that follow to get an insight into some do's and don'ts in your VC attempt. These are some general principles that may not work in every situation. But most of them can prove to be very handy during grueling meetings with seasoned investors. Most of the points that follow have been covered in some form or the other in the previous chapter and have been mentioned here to offer you a simple and easy to use checklist. Lastly, these points are being written assuming that you have followed the steps suggested in the previous chapter and have conducted your due diligence and research well.

1. Be focused while short-listing the VCs you would like to pitch to. In all there would be hundreds of VC firms in the country and you cannot possibly hope to reach out to each one of them. Also, VC firms sometimes have specialties that drive their business model. Some of them may invest only in biotechnology companies while the others may do it for tech stocks. So if you are launching a software company, aim to approach VCs that have a track record of investing in tech start-ups. Meeting an investor from an organization that invests only in biotechnology projects may prove to be a wasted effort.

2. Don't ever ignore the business plan. It is your ticket to a successful fund-raising exercise. I would not repeat the advantages of writing a plan paper again as it has been amply covered in previous chapters. Discipline yourself to prepare that report before you do anything else and you will feel the benefits as soon as you enter the VC track.

3. Remember the 'elevator pitch'? Even at the cost of repetition I feel compelled to remind you about it. It will be the most effective tool in getting you across tables with VC companies. Again, the crucial role of this pitch has been discussed earlier and you will grasp its importance right in your first telephonic conversation with an investor.

4. Try and read a small book on issues like valuations, acquisitions and sweat equity. Although this will not provide you with too much armor against the bankers and VCs who mostly live off this knowledge. However, it will ensure that you do not look blank when such topics are broached upon.

5. If you have been operating a small outfit as a 'proof of concept' before you went out hunting for consolidation/expansion investment, make sure you have your figures and audits in place. VCs are usually very inclined towards numbers, so be ready with them.

6. It is always good to have a list of plausible team members ready with you. If you know well-qualified professionals who you plan to rope in for your venture, have the names and credentials in place.

There is very little you can achieve alone and VCs are aware of that.

7. It might be a good idea to try and get some PR activity in place. A few clippings in the press praising your initiative would not fool any investor. However, it always presents your venture as something that is already on the roll. It's a small psychological advantage but every tiny support mechanism assumes great importance in these situations. Any professional PR company would be able to help you in this regard.

8. Do not ever let the VC representatives feel that you are there to beg them for money. Go with the attitude of a businessperson carrying a value proposition. A venture fund would never give you money just because you were humble, sweet and meek in the meeting. You have to keep in mind that the VC will also eventually make money on the venture and maybe they need you just as much as you need them. In all politeness, you may confess that you are also looking at other Funds. Remember, you are looking for partners, not bosses.

The disadvantages of working with a professional investment fund are hardly worth mentioning. The only drawback (which is sometimes quite serious) is the loss of complete management control. The VC would be a member on your Board and you would have to function a little more democratically. However, I personally do not consider this a disadvantage since all the presence of the VC on your Board will do is to make you function more systematically and introduce accountability even for you. This is a good addition in the long run. In all other ways, this arrangement is a bagful of big and serious advantages for you. Technology and operational know-how, global alliances, industry best practices, mentors - VCs bring in everything. Moreover, even getting business becomes much easier when you have a big Fund's name associated to yours. A multinational might not place an order with you when you approach them independently. On the other hand, they would not hesitate in doing so if you tell them that you are a UBS Warburg backed company.

Venture capital hunt is bound to be an uphill ride for you. However, you must give it your best shot, especially if you are planning an innovative venture. Even if you fail to raise money, this effort is bound to teach you a lot of crucial lessons. It will give you a realistic impression of your plan and will make you a better professional and a more committed entrepreneur.

High Net Worth Individuals - Your Best Bet!

OK, now its time you went and met that rich uncle who drove a Mercedes but you could never really figure out what he actually did to make those riches. For those of you who are slightly unclear about the exact meaning of the term HNI, let me describe the set of people who fall under this category. High Net Worth Individuals are people with large volumes of money that have been passed on to them in legacy or earned by them over their own career spans (technically described as people with above INR 5 crore in assets excluding real estate). These are the people who have the capability of offering start-up finance to entrepreneurial attempts. In very simple words, they are 'loaded' with money. Money that they can do a calculative gamble with. Money that can be the most precious contribution to your business!

About a year and a half back I read an article on the front page of the Sunday magazine of a leading daily, which addressed high net worth individuals. That article beautifully described how a dearth in the availability of high-return investment options for the rich could be overcome by well-planned and evaluated investments into start-up ventures. And why not? I have witnessed more than a score of companies which have shown consistent yearly growth rates above 100% in their first five years of operations. In a scenario where conservative channels of investments refuse to yield anything higher than a measly 6-8%, new ventures with high growth prospects offer a fresh, exciting and fulfilling avenue of making money earn more money. And trust me, I connected completely with the article. This was because during the course of my own corporate career, I have come across numerous such moneyed individuals and I have come to respect their enterprise and willingness to go the extra mile in trying to build further on their existing assets.

To further understand the entire dynamics of HNI investments, lets take a question and answer route. The following are a set of questions which will come very close to your own thinking process and the answers aim to clarify many of those doubts.

Q. *Why would any high net worth individual invest money in my business? Most of the HNIs themselves would be businesspeople. So why won't they just pump more money into their own companies?*

A. All businesses need a certain amount of money at any particular stage. For most HNIs, their existing businesses already have the money required for expansion or diversification plans. The money that you want from them is over and above their corporate and personal requirements. Simply, don't worry about their businesses and how much money they have. Believe me, the depth of most HNIs pockets is really beyond your imaginative horizon. Just know that they have the money and gun for it. Secondly, in today's competitive and unpredictable business world, everyone wants to hedge bets. Stock holding in new and promising ventures offers such security of portfolio to these rich men and women.

Q. *Why do HNIs invest in risky start-ups at all? Why don't they just invest into traditional securities, however low yielding they may be?*

A. I know it is sometimes difficult for a lot of middle-class people, including myself to an extent, to understand what is it like to have so much money where you have almost exhausted all avenues of investment, to a logical level. You have bought houses, farmlands, works of art, cars, government bonds, corporate securities, stock, gold...and you still have a lot of money left! And with all due respect to the law of the land, some of you have bagfuls of cash that you haven't really written down on your income statements. So you either lend money to finance films or invest in potential ventures. Also, I would now give you my opinion of a small psychoanalytical view that I unknowingly bumped into. Making truckloads of money does not guarantee corporate respect. And this is what a lot of HNIs are looking for! I met a gentleman who was one of the largest traders of Cinnamon in India. He had all the money in the world, but he openly admitted to me over dinner that he longed for fame and recognition. This is a feeling shared by a lot of rich and established people who have devoted their lives to their work but are still waiting to figure on The Economic Times front page or address high-level business conferences. And all of them have seen young and bright tech wiz kids hitting headlines with their companies. The need for self-actualization is steep in a lot of moneyed businesspeople and they see investing in 'corporate' start-ups a powerful vent. I know this may sound like a shallow reason, but you will realize its strength when you interact deeply with these people.

Q. *Is investment from HNIs a loan or is it equity participation?*

A. It can be both - based on your need and the form and modalities of investment the investor is looking for. Normally, it is quite easy to raise money in the form of a loan. This is simply because a large number of people with excess cash would be willing to invest it with you as long as they are confident that you would return it to them on time and at the decided interest rate. So in this case you don't really have to do a lot of convincing on how good and potential your business venture is. You just need to instill the faith factor in them, either through common friends, relatives or business associates. A large number of businesses thrive on this form of financing, real estate and industrial trading being two of them. However, as suggested in the previous section, it may not be a very safe bet for you as a young and inexperienced entrepreneur to get money via this route. Just like bank loans, this model would also burden you with repayment obligations right from day one and become a cause for high stress. So try and sell the idea of equity participation to high net worth individuals and make them partners in sharing risks and profits. We will discuss more on this topic in the next section.

Q. *What should I expect from HNIs and what do they expect from my venture in case they make an equity-based investment?*

A. It is important you remember that high net worth individuals are not just rich, they are also extremely well networked. In my own case, the partnership between our investors and us not only brought in high sums of money in the form of equity investment but also drew in a spate of new orders and assignments from the existing market presence of our investors. So make sure that your investors pump in not just money but the years of experience and contacts that they have nurtured through their careers in the corporate and business world. This aspect also justifies why you should target equity participation and make the investors feel like a part of your company's growth. When they are convinced that your venture's success is in sync with their own monetary and social growth, the overall support and attitude of the investors goes through a sea change.

Lets now take a look at your responsibilities towards your shareholders (or equity investors). The foremost rule of building a corporation is to ensure highest possible shareholder value. You must emboss this clearly in your business vision that the people who helped you during your early days in business are the people you owe a lot to. You need to be genuinely concerned and committed towards growth in the stock value of your investors and deliver the promise you made to them while pitching in for funding. If you have told an investor who injected a hundred thousand dollars into your business that he would be able to sell his shares for a million dollars ten years later, then work like a machine to achieve that for your investor. Your success will come by as a natural by-product of your shareholders growth. Secondly, do not go the boo.com way and be very prudent in spending the investors' money. The best approach would be to spend it as if you sold your wife's jewelry to get this cash. Bite every hundred rupees and make them count. Finally, be extremely ethical and honest in your accounts and legalities and ensure that all profits are distributed and decisions are taken collectively.

Q. *How do I approach High Net Worth Individuals?*

A. There is obviously no hard and fast approach that you would use to reach out to prospective investors. Nor can you take the age-old 'cold calling' path. The best and most useful option is to try and remember every rich person you and your family ever knew. Your father's friend, that distant cousin, that relative in New York, rich and friendly neighbors, your tennis partner, acquaintances and associates - all of them can be potential business partners and investors. But first you need to make sure that you have shed all inhibitions in asking for favors! I know how difficult it can be to just call up an uncle you haven't met in ages and tell him you want to talk business. What will he think? What will he say? Before you get into this spiral, let me inform you about something interesting regarding these rich and established people. Almost all of them are very sharp businesspeople who are open and willing to explore new business ideas and enterprising enough to recognize a good deal when it comes by. So if a rich relative has been treating you like a young boy or girl so far, don't think that will happen again when you propose a serious business venture. Most likely you will witness a dramatic change in their way of communicating with you and end up appreciating their commercial and financial acumen. Most seasoned businesspeople have been in need for money sometime or the other in their lives. As a result they respect and understand the situation you are in and would probably encourage you whole heartedly even if they do not find your business suitable to their investment needs. So be fearless and upfront and barge into as many HNIs you can possibly approach. Let the world around you know that you intend to make your fortunes out of an entrepreneurial dream. Remember, even a little baby gets milk only when he/she cries out aloud.

Q. *What is the preparation I need to do before I seriously commence discussions with prospective investors?*

A. There lies a fundamental difference in the approach you need to take when pitching to a venture capital fund and when you do the same with a high net worth individual. This distinction arises simply out of the varying evaluation parameters and investment objectives. A venture capital fund would insist on your professional background. A high net worth individual might just invest in you for the entrepreneurial spark you display. Venture Capital companies and investment banks undertake elaborate due diligence while evaluating your business plan. They would study statistics, market share figures, projections and trends. Most high net worth individuals I have met, refuse to even take a look at these models and spreadsheets. They rely more on their gut feel, experience and business foresight. VC firms have pre-planned investment portfolio decisions which they rarely digress from. HNIs have no such models in place; they invest as and when they come across a profitable proposition. Most importantly, a majority of the VC Funds plays the role of active investors. HNIs are normally passive players who invest in your company and leave the management and operational issues to you. To put things in a nutshell, with HNIs you may not have to prepare those many tables and diagrams but you do have to be ready with answers to some practical and tough questions. Questions that stem from business minds that have implemented several such plans, have seen ups and downs in business and have felt the heat more closely than you can imagine. They may not have read all the management books in the world, but are the true gurus of the art of generating profits.

I hope the above given Q&A session has addressed most of your questions related to private placement of equity. Just a few more lines of advise - out of my own experience with my business and the start-up consulting assignments that I have undertaken, I can confidently state that high net worth individuals around you can be the best resource pool for your venture in case your financing needs fall within the half-million dollar ceiling. Anything above that makes the deal volume high and takes it beyond the comfortable investment zone of most HNIs. In that case you come right back to planning that big VC meeting.

As final preparation for the investment pitch with any HNI, make sure that you have a simply written, jargon-free executive summary of your business plan. Since the gentleman or lady you are approaching would probably not have the technical expertise to appreciate your business operations, there is no use of going into the nitty-gritty of the implementation construct. Concentrate more on simpler (?) issues of revenue streams, business volumes, costs and the strengths and weaknesses of the plan. Do not try and use any of the cosmetics you added to your plan document written for the investment bank or VC Fund. Be realistic, straightforward, crisp and energetic. Note the fact that in the absence of domain expertise and research information, the HNI is most likely to invest in you as a prospect and not your business. In case you have already put in some of your own hard-earned money into the company or you intend to do that soon, make sure to emphasize on this.

The investor would feel much more secure and find his/her money in serious and committed hands. Finally, just like the VC funding architecture, be sure to state clear and present earning and exit options for the investor. The latter could be in the form of profit sharing, director's salary, dividend income or offloading of equity; whichever seems most logical with the business model under consideration. Do not mislead the investor on any front. If you feel you will be able to offer him/her any Return on Investment only after ten years, make it clear at the outset. One of the most important ingredients of corporate growth is harmonious investor relations and a strong foundation for the same should be built right from the first day of association.

Advantages of HNI Investment -

1. As mentioned above, this is clearly the most accessible form of sourcing funds for your start-up venture. Also, the number of HNIs you can hope to approach is much higher than any other alternative like banks or VC organizations.

2. Low complexity investment option. As against bank loans or venture capital, the amount of paperwork, legalities and time frame involved are comparatively negligible. Since you are dealing with an individual and not an institution, the decision-making and the process are much swifter.

3. In case you are looking for freedom of management and operations, HNIs offer you the most suitable choice. They would rarely interfere with your day-

to-day work and at worst would ask you for a copy of your balance sheet at the end of the year.

Disadvantages of HNI Investment -

1. One of the most serious drawbacks of HNI investments is that they do not offer you the brand association strength that most established Funds and Banks do. For example, your organization would be viewed as much more professional and cutting-edge if you have bagged investment from ICICI or Connect Capital. On the other hand a city-based marble trader may provide you with all the money but can never compete with the aforementioned institutions when it comes to a brand comparison.

2. Putting it crudely, private placement with one individual leaves you vulnerable to the whims and fancies of that person. I do not mean to say that these individuals are in any way less professional or competent than their institutional counterparts. However, each one of us would agree that there does lie a serious difference in dealing with an individual and doing the same with an established organization. The latter have policies, procedures and standards that HNIs would not offer.

> **Box 8.** *I remember this extremely interesting meeting I attended with one of my clients who was trying to pitch in to HNIs for investment in his technology consulting company that he wished to launch in the USA. This interview was with one of the biggest builders and real estate developers of the National Capital. Having attended numerous meetings with VC Funds and investment banks, we were*

ready for another eight-round ordeal with this gentleman. The discussion started on a regular model explanation note and moved gradually to the investment figures. The volume of investment we were looking for touched approximately one million USD and we were willing to give away 40% of the company for the same. On offering excel sheets with cost and revenue projections, the gentleman waved his hand and exclaimed in vernacular language that he never sees such tables. Another ten minutes into the meeting and we were convinced that not only was he not interested in the plan, he had almost gone to sleep! Having finished with what we had to say, we were ready to leave yet another futile meeting. Just then the gentleman opened his eyes, turned to his accountant and asked him to release a cheque for 'the kids' worth ten thousand USD in Indian Rupees as the first payment. Trying our best to keep our excitement under wraps we drew his attention to the fact that no papers had been signed so far. To this he simply answered that those were operational issues that could be handled at convenience. He got up, shook hands and left!

That deal did not work out the next day due to equity sharing issues. However, the point to be noted is the ease with which this deal could have materialized. Simply, when it comes to deal closure, an HNI investment surpasses all other options in terms of speed and convenience. The reasons are obvious. When dealing with High Net Worth Individuals, you need to convince and negotiate with one person. In all other options you need to convince a Board. Clearly, the former turns out to be an easier alternative.

The Role of Investment Banks

Ever wondered what magnificent names like JM Morgan Stanley, DSP Merill Lynch, Kotak Mahindra and UBS Warburg actually do? They are what are lovingly called the 'dealmakers' of the corporate sector. Ranging from all areas of corporate finance, mergers and acquisitions and disinvestments deals, these banks also offer services including the areas of fund-raising, IPOs and strategic alliances. They form the critical bridge between two organizations or parties intending to do business together (e.g. an entrepreneur and an investor). Investment Bankers usually offer a one-stop-shop for legal and corporate consulting, financial management, investor search road shows and global alliances. Often referred to as the 'sharks' or 'hawks', these bankers represent a personification of core business knowledge, diligent research, dedicated client support, sharp communication abilities and tremendous patience with spreadsheets. From my personal experience of dealing with Bankers, I can forcefully confess that it is always better to have Bankers on your side than have them against you.

How can your venture draw any mileage out of the presence of these organizations? Frankly not much if you are looking at the kind of big names mentioned above. Organizations like those and others like HSBC, Deutsche Bank and Citibank normally handle deals with much higher transaction sizes than you are probably planning to start with. From my basic understanding I can suggest that even a million dollar plan may not be too exciting for any of these big shops. However, there are plenty of smaller, yet equally professional outfits that may suit your venture size. Examples of these can be Waygate Capital Partners, Westbridge Capital, Avendus Advisors, Asia One and many more. My own Company has worked with two of these institutions on a deal and we thoroughly profited through the association. Glance through the bullet points that follow to get a clear understanding of how an Investment Bank can go a long way in assisting you raise funds for and launch your company -

1. You can approach Investment Banks directly and discuss your business plan with them. It may be an uphill task to get them interested in you venture since most Banks would be keener to help you with second round of funding and private placement than when you are just starting out. However, you need not get disheartened and try anyway. Banks also need a regular 'deal flow' to stay in business and you may catch them with an attractive proposition where the Bank sees value.

2. Investment Banks work on either 'mandate fee' and/or 'success fee'. If you are a first generation entrepreneur with just a few thousands in your pocket, you can most likely forget about the first option. A mandate fee simply means that although the Bank will assist you with all it resources and intent, it does not guarantee you success and will charge you for the consulting and assistance provided. Not out of choice but compulsion, the success fee model would suit you better. Here success would mean achievement of pre-defined fund raising or alliance goal. In this case you will pay the Bank for its services only once you are able to raise resources for your venture. A lot of mid-sized Banks would be able to offer you such an arrangement. In a worse scenario you could try and work out a combination of a small mandate fee and a much larger success fee

chunk. This will not only help the Bank cover some of its costs incurred on your deal but also prove your seriousness about the whole exercise.

3. The biggest advantage of working with a Bank is that once you have convinced them and they begin work on your venture, you can rest assured about the professionalism, width of investor outreach, truly value-adding alliances, strategic consulting and overall corporate penetration. Moreover, your credibility takes a quantum jump when you approach a prospective investor backed by an Investment Bank. Your passion, boundless energy and feeling for your start-up clubbed with the razor-sharp pitch of your Bankers would be powerful enough to impress any investor, as long as all this is underpinned with a solid business model.

The above write-up may have portrayed a starry picture of working with Investment Banks. I admit it is starry - provided you get to partner a Bank. I feel compelled to emphasize the difficulty you may face in convincing a Bank to take up your case especially in the scenario when you cannot pay them any mandate fee and their money would be earned only on successful implementation of the fund-raising plan. More so if you are a technology start-up, since the spate of investments pumped into tech ventures during the last few years has forced venture funds to reduce exposure to technology and thus makes investor search tough even for established investment banks. What you do need to remember while negotiating with Investment Banks is that although the evaluation parameters of your business model will be the same, there is a glaring difference between the way you pitch to a venture fund and when you do the same with a Bank. Banks would be service providers and you will be the client, however small. Keeping this in mind and the fact that smaller banks are equally eager to get deals working, you really don't need to be in a sales-pitch gear when working out an arrangement. If you approach these banks with a serious value proposition and a plan that not only gives them a fair chance to earn money but also add to their portfolio of reputed deals, your chances of cracking an association would increase manifold. Be confident, sure and professional about your venture and follow most of the rules mentioned for venture capital interviews. The rest would be much easier.

There are numerous websites that will be able to guide you to the right Bank in case you need to zero down on the organizations that can help you. A little advice even at the cost of repetition - do not spend too much time in trying to get one of the top Investment Banks on your side. They would almost certainly not be interested but your attempt to reach them and convince them would just eat up a lot of your precious time. Aim for smaller shops that have dealt in your domain previously and whose mandate fee would not require you to sell off your house and car.

Having read everything mentioned above, keep in view the day when you would be running a $100 million world-class organization. On that day you would not have to look for any Investment Bankers. They will look for you.

Proof of Concept for Investor Confidence

Leaving aside whatever we have read in the previous sections, let us just take a quick pragmatic view of this entire investment raising activity. Put yourself in an investor's shoe and think carefully - how would you finally select the ventures you would want to fund? What would it really take to make you take a decision? A smart and flashy young man in a crisp suit, with a well-written business plan, a good MBA degree and a twang in his accent? I don't think so. And most real investors don't think so either. So what is it that will truly enthuse confidence into a prospective investor? What is it that will offer tangible proof of your projections and revenue model? The answer lies in what software professionals call a 'working prototype'.

A venture capital company wrote an interesting email to me a couple of years back. The mail had a simple suggestion - turn your two-member organization to a twenty-member organization on your own and then we will help you become a two hundred-member company. The message was very clear. The investors wanted me to take the slow tough road to entrepreneurial growth and then look for force-multipliers to steep up that curve. And that seems to be quite a fair expectation. It becomes much easier to look for investors once you have built up an organization, however small, and are doing profitable business, however low in volume. I will give you an example. Suppose you wish to launch a training and education company in the area of fashion designing. You intend to follow the franchise network model of business and plan to open at least three centers each in all big cities and towns of India. You intend to keep the course planning and quality control centralized. The edge that you offer in your new course is the advanced textile and fabric marketing clubbed with designing training. You have also conducted a thorough research on the scope of growth, industry trends, competitor matrix and market analysis and it all points well towards an untapped opportunity. And now you need investment to realize this ambitious plan. The volume of investment you are gunning for touches almost a million dollars that you need over the first two years of operations. However, most of the investment you are looking for is for ad spends and promotions that together form the deadliest combination to burn rapidly through your cash. Moreover, no matter how powerful your plan looks on paper, there is really no guarantee of its success. Such big volumes of money in the start-up stage, half of it for advertising and no existing infrastructure or organization to support it - it really has to be one hell of an optimistic investor to give you the money!

On the other hand, lets focus on the prototype mentioned above taking the same example. Now consider a case where you have approached the same investor with the same business plan, but only after you have successfully test-fired it on one unit. Which means that you have launched one center (or maybe two), implemented all your models on it and are already in a revenue inflow mode, if not profits. You have built up reasonable infrastructure, finalized on your training pedagogy, material and manuals, recruited faculty, conducted local promotions and finally converted prospective students to a full-fledged running batch. You have learnt the fundamentals of managing an educational institution, along with the skills and tactics to sell it. If you have been able to forge alliances with strategic partners (for student placement, global exchange programs, foreign certifications or R&D), it will add more teeth to your venture. All the above together will go a long way in proving the marketability of your model along with providing a good reference point for analyzing the scalability of the same. Most importantly, it will prove your professional ability as an individual to conceptualize, launch and run an organization with minimal resources. It will prove your entrepreneurial mettle. Now imagine all the aforementioned achievement under your sleeve when you approach the investor. Not only will the investor take you more seriously, you will also notice a sudden jump in your own confidence and conviction about the business model. Secondly, you will now be looking for an impetus to your existing business and not angel funds to help you stand up. This will reflect in every word you say and investors are too sharp to miss it.

Once your prototype is studied and assessed by the prospective investor, it is bound to generate higher response levels. At this stage the investors feel they are negotiating with an organization and not just with a dreamy individual. Your accounts and balance sheets will offer first-hand insight into the financials of your venture, which will assist in projecting future costs and revenues. Overall, it is the same old principle of 'seeing is believing' that works here too. This holds true for both institutional and individual investors since the basic parameters and psyche behind an investment decision do not vary too much. So the lesson is simple. Try and build an organization on a shoestring budget and commence operations with a view to break-even and gather market learning. Do not get disheartened if you are unable to achieve the scale that you had initially planned. Treat this entire exercise as a critical part of your build-up stage and something that will provide you with the key intellectual capital to give shape to your ultimate plan. Don't get too worried if you are not in a profit zone already. Remember, even Amazon.com took a long time to clock its first penny of profit.

You must be thinking that all that is written above makes sense, but where do you get even the little money required to launch that small outfit initially. The obvious answer is that you do it with your own money. With this we arrive at the painful aspect of putting in your hard-earned savings into the risky proposition of business. How much money can you pump into your enterprise to start with? How long can you keep doing it? Where do you arrange it? These are some of the questions we will attempt to study in the next section.

Self-Financing

I have come across very few business people who have not had to risk their personal money during their entire business life. At some stage or the other even the most established enterprise leaders have to grope into their own pockets for bailing their company out during a financial crisis. And the scary part is that some of them even lose it! What differs smart entrepreneurs from failed business people is the fine balance that needs to be struck between personal financial security and risk appetite. This also with an understanding of when is the right moment to inject the money and when it should be taken out. Why, even Henry Ford went bankrupt at the age of 45, only to bounce back and give this world the revolutionary assembly line and finally become Time Magazine's Man of the Century.

Lets now define what we exactly mean by self-financing. Self-financing refers to the money that you personally arrange for your start-up enterprise. This could be your own savings made over your previous career span, funds borrowed from parents, relatives and friends, finance organized through liquidating property or real estate and some people go all the way including their wives' jewelry under this category (which is most certainly not advisable!). And most businesses in this world probably began with the help of the few coins an entrepreneur brought to the table. Some entrepreneurs began this way and later sought financial support and some carried on with their own revenue accruals.

We must together shatter a myth that leads to most entrepreneurial ideas being given up right in the cradle. This myth is that launching a business venture takes a lot of money irrespective of the nature of domain. As you may know by now, HCL started in a small rooftop shack in New Delhi. Today it is one of the most powerful and respected Information Technology companies of India. One of the largest placement services company in Mumbai began its operations from a small room and a telephone line ten years back. Subrata Roy of the great Sahara India Pariwar himself launched para-banking on a very humble note. Today he has built what is called 'India's wealthiest family'. Jeff Bezos of Amazon once delivered books door-to-door in his own car and today is one of the most well known corporate personalities worldwide. So the point is that although some businesses certainly are capital intensive, the others are not. For example, if you wish to launch a human resources placement services company, the infrastructure can very conveniently be restricted to a small room taken on rent, a telephone line, a computer, a table and a few chairs. Maybe you can add to it a small marketing and promotions budget. So while your marketing campaign with brochures, mailers and stationary would not exceed a few thousand rupees, all the other heads taken together would probably cost you another fifty thousand. In all you would need to cough up a lakh of rupees to get your business going. In today's times this amount is not very unreasonable or scary. And if you are a smart individual with some business acumen, you will earn this money back within three months.

Please study the following guidelines before you decide to fund your own venture -

1. Do not liquidate key assets unless available in surplus. Simply, do not sell your only house, your only car and your wife's jewelry. Business is not about rushing into risk. It's about calculating it and cautiously planning for it.

2. However embarrassed you may feel, do not shy away from borrowing money from your father or close relatives. As long as you honestly intend to repay them, there can be no other worthier cause to borrow.

3. Plan for both capital expenses (one time set-up

expenses) and working capital (the money you need on a daily or monthly basis). I have witnessed many entrepreneurs who invest all their money in the first month and then suffer from serious funds shortage in the subsequent months. Remember, all businesses experience gestation periods - the lag time between investing and the first penny of profits. So make sure you keep away enough funds to see you through your gestation period, whether it is one week or one year.

4. Spend money on high utility items before any luxury expenses. Make sure you print your business cards before you buy that painting for your office.

5. If you plan to use your own savings for the venture, that would be the most ideal form of self-financing. However, try not to pour in all your savings in one go. Businesses are uncertain for at least the initial phase and you need to retain some money for the rainy day.

By now I hope I have been able to address most of the issues that arise when an entrepreneur is looking out for that one little push to get him or her going. I must mention that none of the suggestions or phenomena written about in this chapter has universal applicability. Nor do I claim one hundred per cent accuracy in the evaluations made while discussing financing options. At the end of this section I would only like to convey that do not let financial hurdles play a bigger role than they actually should. Most committed entrepreneurs I have met were able to raise money for their dream venture one-way or the other. And so will you! All you need is an HB pencil, a sheet of paper, a will that burns like fire, some mid-night oil and eyes full of dreams. After all, we just need to remember what Socrates once said "When you want success like you want air to breathe, you are bound to get it."

❋ ❋ ❋ ❋ ❋ ❋ ❋ ❋ ❋ ❋ ❋ ❋ ❋

Starting your Start-up

Preparing for the battle

The stage is set. You have finalized your business plan, conducted research, have a grip on the competitive scenario, have incorporated a private limited company and have the investment to get started. However, you are still all alone and you possibly cannot hope to single-handedly launch and run your start-up company. You now need to build an organization around you and your business plan. Even if your business model is primarily based on your own professional skill set (for example Consultancy), you would still need to set up the basic infrastructure, office or manufacturing space, equipment, stationary, printed material and most of all - people. What does an infantry platoon do before they fire the first shell towards the enemy? They polish their gun barrels, gather ammunition dumps, dig trenches and use camouflage. The situation for you and your leap into the fiery competitive arena demands similar preparation. This chapter will discuss the fundamentals of bringing together a small or medium sized organization and the steps you need to follow to be able to do that in the smartest, quickest and most cost-effective way.

We will divide our discussion into four 'P's of building an organization - People, Premises, Procedures and Positioning. You will notice that most of the activities that you do to gear up your start-up to hit the market will be permutations and combinations of these four heads. Let us start with the first and by far the foremost resource of an organization - its people.

Recruiting People - The Deciding Factor

I have no doubt in my mind while I mention this again and again - an organization is not made successful by any brand, any amount of money or any innovation. It is made successful only as an outcome of the quality and effort of its people. It is people who innovate. Innovations lead to superior products. Superior products lead to profits. Profits lead to marketing spends and brand building. Finally, good brands attract better people and the cycle goes on. But this cycle always has to begin with the people.

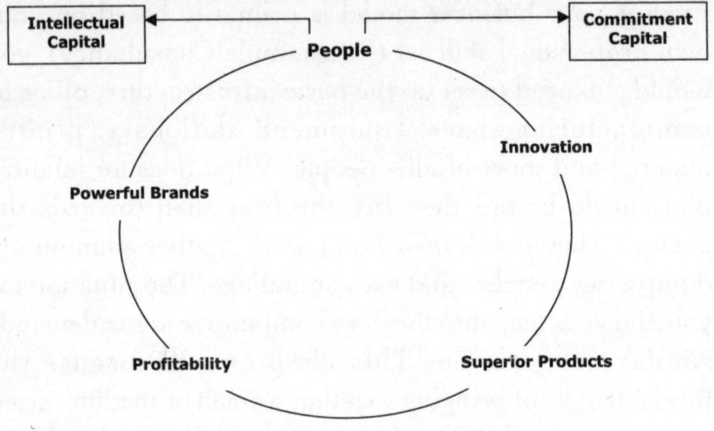

The above diagram simply depicts the foundation that the initial few people lay towards the building of an organization. Although the human resource of an organization always plays a critical role in the functioning of a company irrespective of its size and establishment, the responsibility assumes astronomical proportions during the start-up stage. It is the set of people who begin work with an organization during its formative years who leave footprints of excellence, commitment and intrapreneurship behind, to be followed by the people who join in later. The first few employees or team members of a young new company not only form the second line of management of the organization in the years to come but also form the fountainhead of a work culture, collective goals and ethics within and outside the company. They are the face of the company for the newly acquired clients, the team that faces maximum resource crunch, work out of the barest infrastructure, play both the roles of managers and workers, train every new entrant of the team, deeply understand the strengths and weaknesses of the company and share a special bond with the promoters of the venture. In short, the first few recruits you get can make or break your dream company. Remember, a company can never survive on investments. Companies grow through profit lines that are built on sustained intellectual and commitment capital of their people.

So how do you choose these people? More importantly, how do these people choose you? You will obviously not be able to pay them even close to industry standards. You don't have a big brand to attract people just for Resume value. And you will probably club it all with inhuman working conditions. Overall, it will be a big challenge for you. So is there really no way of gathering a few good people? Is monetary compensation the only incentive that can be offered? Or is there anything else that may make up for the lower figures? There is. If you cant offer them money or position, offer them some honest dreams.

Offer dreams to hard bred professionals? Sounds more like a Hollywood story punch line right? Think again.

If this was not true, no start-up company would have ever been able to recruit talented individuals and entrepreneurial stories would not have painted the whole of Silicon Valley. Have you ever thought about what ESOPs or Employee Stock Options are? A lot of small, medium and large IT companies offer ESOPs to its employees as rewards and incentives. The reason is that the Management of these companies wants to make these people partners in success and failure. These stock options are normally never too high priced at the time they are offered. They only carry a promise - a collective dream.

Understanding Different Needs of Different People

I sometimes wish all of us entrepreneurs had done a course on human psychology back in school. But now that most of us haven't, we can at least try and get an insight into the way different kinds of people plan career maps and what drives whom. Every individual has a different and unique set of aspirations and you need to look out for those who aim to get what you can offer - in both short and long terms. I have personally interviewed over two hundred people during my short career span. With the little experience I have been able to gather doing that, I can safely divide them into two categories based purely on their suitability for start-up companies. The first category belongs to those who come with an 'I am looking for a safe job with a safe company' approach. The other section comprises people who believe in the 'I am here for a high-return, long-term career' perspective. It is the latter category that you need to hunt for. Understand this, every individual has a goal to achieve in his or her lifetime.

Obviously, some people are more ambitious than the others. What you carefully need to look for are people who have the willingness to take a few calculated risks now with a view to achieve extraordinary growth later. I will give you an example of a real-life case that happened in my own company. When we started out, we recruited two bright young people for business development. Both were hardworking, talented and well educated. However, their temperaments and career plans differed diametrically. One of them made it clear in his actions and words that he was in the company to see it through the difficult times and reap the benefits years later. The other wanted just a regular job. A time came when business became tough and the going was bumpy. The second man quit immediately and joined an established real estate company as a sales executive. The first stuck on and worked as a committed team member even during months when even salaries were delayed. Today, he is a Vice President in our company with fifteen professionals reporting to him. He earns a lot of money and drives a shining car. The second individual is still struggling as a sales executive and has seen little growth in that real estate company.

The point is straight. Look for people who are willing to face the trade-off between job security and meteoric growth. There are numerous such people around and you only need to identify them. We all have heard of the high-flying consultants and techies who left established organizations and jumped into high innovation start ups during the dot com wave. These men and women are still looking for challenging opportunities where they get more than just a nine to five job. And your start-up can be an excellent nursery to groom such sparks.

As usual, here are some secrets to successful employment exercises. They promise to work in some cases and fall flat in the others. The ratio of success would depend on the kind of people you are aiming to bring on board. The 'offering dreams' concept works here also. The points that follow will hopefully explain it well.

1. Identify the exact qualification or experience that you are looking for. Conduct some basic research on the industry standards of compensation for these credentials. If you belong to the same industry, you will probably have an idea already.

2. Get your working capital calculation in place and apportion the amount you can for wage bills. Make sure you spend more on salaries of your people than anything else since they are the bloodstreams of your company. This holds true not only for the services sector but also manufacturing and primary economic activities.

3. Before you advertise in the employment magazines (if you have the money) or get in touch with any placement consultants, look hard around yourself. You are bound to locate talent floating all over. Your best friend, that bright junior from B-School, a cousin, an ex-colleague, the neighbor who solved your computer problem, the salesman who sold you your car…just anyone who shows professional ability and promise. The advantages in this case will be clear. Firstly, you would have known these people outside the interview room and that would help you judge their real self better. Secondly, you would be on a

better communication platform with these people and that would give you a better opportunity to convey your business vision. Thirdly, any bond apart from pure professional relationship would assist in offering longevity to this association. Finally, you will save money on employment magazines and placement consultants.

4. As far as possible, try and recruit fresh graduates and post graduates. The benefits again would be manifold. Fresh recruits can be molded into a work culture since they come with no pre-set mindsets. The second advantage is more practical. Professionals with previous work experience have very sound knowledge about the benefits that they should get from a company. And believe me, your young organization will be able to offer none of those. I had once recruited an engineer from a leading software company. He was very good but found coffee-vending machines to be a prerequisite for a development lab. We were more used to coffee from a local shop. Lastly, fresh graduates come with boundless energy. And as I had mentioned earlier, your venture would need as many injections of adrenalin as possible.

5. Always interview prospects in your own premises even if you are operating out of a dingy cable-manufacturing shed in an industrial area. There should be no 'gap' in the perception of your company and the real picture. A newly funded consulting company once went for campus recruitment to an established management institute. Three candidates were selected on campus with joining dates in the next

week. All three joined a few days later and were shocked to see a two-bedroom house converted into an office space! All three resigned on the same day. The flaw was not in the company. The flaw was in the perception that they had created during their pre-placement lectures in the institute.

6. Be honest about the resource crunch and financial strength or weakness of the company when you meet prospective candidates - but don't go overboard. You should tell them about the hardships they might face during their first few months of work but make sure you also inform them about projected business and how that would change things. Secondly, there is no real need to disclose your bank statement to any new employee, however sincere. Most likely you will have a really low figure to talk about and that may fail to instill confidence into a new member. So look and sound confident of your company's position and convinced that times would change for the better soon. And trust me, they will.

7. Avoid recruiting people who negotiate salary figures too long. Although there is nothing professionally wrong in that, it does convey an inclination towards monetary compensation as the single most important decision criterion. Even if you do go out of the way in enhancing the figures for such an individual, you can never rest assured that he would not hop into another organization on a marginal jump in salary figures.

8. Have a keen eye on the family background of the

person you recruit. This may sound like a very conservative advice, but I can assure you of its real importance. There is really no logic or explanation behind this concept - only the wisdom passed on by senior corporate achievers and a little experience. Attempt to bring on board men and women from cultured, educated and professionally oriented families and you will perceive the difference instantly. Cultured families imbibe into their children valuable qualities like loyalty, dedication, honesty, warmth and camaraderie. These are all things that go a long way in determining the relationship of an individual with your organization.

9. Unless your work requires some very serious intellectual capital, don't get too bogged down with degrees and qualifications. Look out for talent, communication skills, energy, loyalty, temperament and a willingness to learn. All technical and operational knowledge can be imparted to a promising individual but no dramatic attitudinal changes can be engineered by even the best of managers. I am not saying that motivating team members will not work. It always does. What I mean is that inherently motivated teams are more effective in all business situations and I would personally vote for attitude over technical competence.

10. When you are interviewing people for a start-up, don't ever imagine that you are the evaluator. While you are busy judging people - they are busy judging your company. So use the interview minutes not only to

study candidates but to also 'pitch' to the really brilliant ones. With lack of market presence and no brand penetration of your company, your interface with people becomes the only advertising medium. If you notice big companies place lucrative recruitment ads in employment journals to attract the best talent pool. Now that you cant do the same, make sure that you talk about the strength of the business model, the future growth prospects, value for human resource and the steep compensation increase curve while at the interview...make them dream your dream. That will go a long way in determining the opinion these bright professionals will develop about you.

Be cautious while deciding the total strength of your team. Recruit only the number without which things threaten to come to a grinding halt. Wage bills can be one of the biggest causes of high 'burn rates' and you need to watch out against it. Initially, don't hesitate to plan your team with multiple role allocation. The lady who does the client servicing can also manage the customer help desk. The sales force can look into the accounts. The technicians can clean the machines, the software professionals can become network administrators and every one can get up for their own water and coffee. Keeping a smart and slim outfit right from the beginning will not only allow you to manage your cash flow better but also develop a culture for optimum utilization of organizational resources.

The above discussion is an attempt to give you an insight into recruitment pangs that start-up companies face and some remedies for the same. What you really need to remember is that bringing people on board is still the easier end of the band. Retaining them is the real challenge. We will study the management of people and retention strategies later in the book.

Setting Up the Infrastructure - The Bare Essentials

Jeff Bezos, the celebrated founder of the great Amazon.com was once asked by a newspaper reporter as to why the office of Amazon used plastic coffee cups and cheapest possible pencils despite being a global company. Jeff simply replied, "So that every penny saved here can be used to buy better servers, more T3 lines and thus more customer value". Get the point?

The capital expenses you make should be a calculated blend of bangs for every buck, fulfillment of necessities and basic comfort for you and your team. I distinctly remember the time when we made the most of our very humble infrastructure during the first six to eight months of our company. It makes the whole team nostalgic thinking about the days when we spread white sheets on the floor and sat down around them to make up for the lack of white boards and conference tables in our office. Windows and doors were swung open in case of electricity failures since we had no power back-ups. We borrowed ice from our neighboring offices since we refused to spend money on a refrigerator and if a good number of clients came in all at once, some of our people would have to take a walk since we didn't have enough chairs to seat all of them together. Today all this sounds almost humorous. But when we think deeply about those tough days we overcame, it instills us with a sense of achievement, confidence and satisfaction. That is the true essence of an entrepreneurial struggle.

Take a quick look at the points that follow to plan your spending and setting up in a more systematic and informed way.

1. Do not think of buying real estate with the initial capital you have. I have met some entrepreneurs who believe that buying of office space or a factory would offer them some stability. This is a conservative pattern of planning and modern corporate outlook advocates spending under more 'performing' heads. Secondly, your team strength is bound to increase rapidly and any space that you may buy now will prove to be small in no time. Look out for a rented space in a location that comes closest to your geographical area of work and falls strictly within your budget. In any case, posh offices in business centers are not a distant dream for most ambitious and smart entrepreneurs.

2. Follow the principle of installments and compound interest here also. Almost everything you may want to procure for your company can be bought on installments - computers, mobile phones, machinery, furniture, air conditioners, trucks, lorries and even raw material. Buying on credit may not give you the satisfaction of immediate ownership, but will assist your cash flow management tremendously. First of all you may not even have the money to buy every infrastructure need upfront. Even in case you do it may be prudent to hold back money with yourself as long as possible to feed your recurring expense needs and see you through the gestation period.

3. Buying equipment on second sale may not be a very good plan but you can be selective about it. It is a good idea to scan the market for any great deals that may come by. I know of a plastic pre-form processing company that started out by buying a second hand Swiss blowing machine at throw away prices through a distress sale by the first owner. The machine was in good shape and offered high utility during the first crucial year of operations. On the other hand, do not be too hasty in buying computer hardware in a rush as computers depreciate in value at a mind-blowing pace. As far as possible buy one machine when you think you may need two. By the time you really start missing the second machine, the prices may have fallen and configurations may have changed.

4. In case your work demands people to sit for long hours, get your office air-conditioned. This might sound like a luxury suggestion but is being offered only after substantial experience. Ever thought why some of the developed countries have regulations forcing controlled temperature at workplaces? You may not agree right now but you will discover that the increase in productivity of your people when working in a comfortable environment more that offsets the expenses you incur on providing the same. During the first year of our company we actually faced a resignation by a teammate who could not bear the scorching Delhi heat. We have now ensured that our people love stepping into office during those hellish summer months.

5. Expenditure on fancy furniture, decorative paintings, coffee vending machines, hidden lighting, carpeted flooring and expensive mobile phones are a strict no-no. Although all this would be simple common sense which you probably understand anyway. However, the first few post-investment days (in case you are not working out of your own money) are very dangerous since they give you a strong 'loaded' feeling. You need to watch out when this happens. You need to remember that this money has to last till your company starts getting its own accruals from the market. So save all this money for that really bad month waiting for you with open jaws a few months down the line.

6. Do not compromise on some essentials like business cards for your customer-facing people, purified drinking water, telephone lines (at least two) and a well-lit work place. On the other hand you should well avóid expenses like office helpers, expensive stationary, conference tables and sofas. In any case, you will be the best judge in prioritizing these expense heads based on your business model and the perception you want to generate. For example, I am aware of some multi-level marketing companies where the Promoters just have to invest in flashy cars and cell phones to create a market wave about the success of their plans. This word-of-mouth is their strongest business development tool. So evaluate your needs on all the parameters that affect your business and take a systematic route towards skinning every rupee.

7. There should be no hesitation in spending money on

compliance with the law of the land. For example, if your work requires software packages (which it most probably will), buy only licensed software. This may be a head you haven't budgeted for, but whether it is accounting software like Tally or simply MS Office, you don't want compliance officers and Nasscom reps knocking on your door in a few weeks. In any case, use of pirated software is an unethical practice and it is logical not to indulge in it.

8. If your work is labor intensive, for example a manufacturing unit or a garment export house, make sure the manpower work in neat and ventilated spaces with regular supply of refreshments. It also might be a good idea to set up a small canteen where the workforce can revitalize their mind, body and spirit. It need not be too elaborate and can be made in a corner of your premises. Similarly, if you were in a perishable products business like food processing, it would be foolish to try and save money on infrastructure components like warehousing and storage.

9. Bargain, bargain, bargain! Whenever you step out into the market to buy any product or service for your company, bargain like a hawk. Very widely accepted business sense says that you make money on buying and not selling. This obviously follows the adage 'a penny saved is a penny earned' and can be very useful in your attempt to save every penny possible. I remember sitting in one of my investor's office while he was speaking to two different computer vendors negotiating the best price for a laptop computer.

Seeing him haggle for a mere two thousand rupees made me wonder as to why a man of his stature and riches would do so. At the end of the call he could see my amused facial expression. He candidly told me that talking on the phone for five minutes just saved him a couple of thousand rupees. He laughed and stated "nothing else I do can make me earn two thousand in five minutes". He was so right.

All of the above-mentioned points fall completely under the common sense set. However, having met numerous entrepreneurs who face financial crunch due to overspending or spending on wrong areas in their initial few months, I felt this read might be value-adding (or value-saving!) for you. Even if this won't make any dramatic impact on your business spending, it will at least provide a collection of thoughts and reminders for you.

It is important for you to understand and believe that you will always have a better grip on your requirements and financial position than any external consultant or observer. So it is impossible to follow any fixed best practices to set up the physical presence of your company. Most likely none of the aforementioned suggestions would be needed if you are working out of your own hard-earned money. Just remember that even when you are utilizing the funds given to you by investors you need to follow the same restraint as you would have when spending from your own pocket. Finally just remember the well-known saying - Not what you read, what you remember makes you wise. And not what you earn, what you save makes you rich!

* * * * * * * * * *

That First One Year

Guts and Glory

You may be asking yourself as to why I am discussing the first one year of operations with you when this book is only about launching a start-up enterprise. Now think about how many times have you seen a company that started with a bang and within a very short time ended up in the graveyard of failed enterprises? How many dot coms perished within six months and how many Indian call centers that mushroomed with a promise to transform the BPO industry worldwide are still alive? How many manufacturing units are set up in industrial areas and how many of them face closures even before the first product line gets sold? The answer lies in the simple observation that most new organizations find themselves in troubled waters or even shut shop in their very first year of active work. If they manage to see this critical period through they go on for a very long time. The causes for this will be highlighted in the next section. The only purpose of penning these lines is to ensure that all you wannabe entrepreneurs get the essence of successful business planning right at the outset - the real challenge is not in starting a business, it is in keeping it alive and running it profitably for years to come. And the first year lays the platform for a start-up to become a respected corporation one day.

If the launch stage will test your planning and organization capabilities, these four quarters will try you a lot more. If you have heard of words like perseverance, determination, stress management, optimism, sacrifice and keeping the faith, these months would make you understand the true meaning of all these. In fact it is this time in your business life that will hold the promise of your evolution from a novice to a reasonably seasoned businessperson. And I can assure you that it will be a test of your nerves involving a lot of pain, tense moments, slogging and a lot of prayers. I don't intend to scare you at this juncture when you have made up your mind to tread the path of struggle and success (...and you have almost read a whole book on it!) but only to make you cautious about the fact that just being able to gather funds, people, plans and infrastructure cannot be taken as tools enough to ensure that you reach for the stars that you wish to. The real battle will begin at the word 'GO'! And why should you fear anything anyway? My dear father once told me - can a rock become a beautiful statue if it fears the strike of a chisel? Can a piece of land be cultivated for fulfilling crop if it fears the plough? This year will be your plough and chisel. Think about it.

But why is the first one year so important? What is so different about this year from the other routine years of normal business life? Ask yourself - why is the first lap of a Formula One race so important even for Michael Schumacher? Why are the first ten overs of a one-day cricket match the deciding factor and why the initial few seconds of a satellite launch determine its successful trajectory? All these rules apply equally and more to business organizations. Let us now take a look at some of the visible and evident turbulences that most start-up organizations are likely to face during their first one year and what makes the latter so different from routine business years.

1. Your company will have no market presence, very few customers and negligible revenue coming in during this period. This obviously means that you would get no business through referrals and word-of-mouth like most organizations with a few years of work behind them do. When there are no primary clients there will be no repeat business and every penny that you earn will have to be an outcome of concentrated sales effort.

2. Most probably you would not have managed a whole organization on your own previously and this inexperience will show. Face it. There is really nothing wrong in admitting that you will be right at the beginning of the entrepreneurial learning curve when you start out. As a result you will take time in learning the inside story of cash flows, people management, collections and even client prospecting. So apart from the setbacks normal business will have to offer, your own education will also play a role.

3. The human resource of your organization will be fresh as daisies when it comes to a company's intellectual capital base. There would be few things that you would be able to call your competitive advantage or your core competence and the first year will be spent trying to discover or develop both of the above.

4. You may have heard about terms like 'business practices', 'trade secrets' and 'organizational policy'. You would not have identified and finalized any of these when you are busy rolling out your business. There is nothing much that you can do anyway as

these are all essential components of the concept of market learning discussed in the previous chapters. For example, you would not be able to determine which debt can be declared as a bad one and which one is just a delayed payment. Personally, by the time I was able to determine the difference I had already lost over ten thousand USD for my company.

5. As Murphy states - when a thing can go wrong, it will! You are bound to face issues of shocking resignations, bad sales months, defaulted payments, crashed hard disks, irate customers, unreasonably disconnected telephones, investor unrest and accounting mismatches. Although all of these are part of 'normal business years', you will surely get bogged down by these (and you should) and lose precious business hours. By the time you get used to such regular hitches you would be in the third year of your entrepreneurial life. I remember an entrepreneur friend calling me at midnight because he had lost an essential piece of his data. Years later he still calls me for rescue - but with significantly less urgency.

6. Finally, everything is related to the volume of products and services you can sell and selling will be the toughest thing to do. Imagine that you visit a prospect and on being asked about your previous experience in offering the same product you just have to disclose that this would be your first attempt! A client would almost feel like a guinea pig and thus getting your first few customers will be an uphill task.

You are bound to face all or at least most of the above

during your first year in business. One year used here repeatedly just denotes an approximate time frame and is not any empirically tested unit. It is normally the time an organization takes to be able to stand up on its own feet. It is also a good measurement bracket, as at the end of this time you will prepare your first balance sheet and profit and loss accounts. So what is the strategy to be adopted during this time to ensure smooth going for the company? If all new organizations face the same challenge irrespective of their size and business domain, how is it that some of them take-off well by the second year and the others face even survival issues? We will now use the next few pages to address these questions and also arrive at suggested plans of action for certain key areas of your organization to effectively overcome the teething troubles.

Training, Leadership and Motivation

I was once surprised to know that Subrata Roy, the founder of the Sahara India Pariwar, participates in the training and development exercises of new entrants into the company even now. His philosophy is simple. Since the Pariwar (or the Family) has been built by people, the new work force has not only to be warmly absorbed into the family but also trained on the key guiding principles and ideologies that have developed Sahara from a once small beginning into one of India's biggest business houses. Great companies like Wipro, GE, TCS and Infosys spend millions of dollars every year in the development of their people. The reason is well understood and has been discussed in previous chapters. People being a company's single most important resource have to be nurtured - both in terms of knowledge training and organizational systems.

But isn't formal training the domain of only established and resource rich companies? Absolutely not. Imparting formal training programs are equally essential for your start-up company and should be one of the areas where you spend maximum time during the first few weeks. But training programs are conducted by professional trainers in any field and should we spend precious resources on organizing such a forum? First of all remember this - your company has an excellent trainer on whom you don't have to spend extra dollars. That trainer is you! And why not? Who can convey the real business sense behind the initiative better than you can? Who would have more research base on your business space than you? Most importantly, in whose eyes will the new people see clearer dreams? Training is not just about educating the recruits about the roles, responsibilities and technicalities. It is about bringing them closer to the organization's vision. In a case where some technical and operational training has to be imparted through experts on the subjects, you must not try to save costs here. A quality training session will bring back all your coins to you ten-fold within no time.

What's more important to understand is that training people can never happen in just an organized seminar room for a few hours or days. Training and development of your people will be an on-going process that would take several formal and informal sessions. I noticed this in one of the most brilliant people and aggressive entrepreneurs I have ever met. This gentleman is heading a huge e-business application services company that he built over just five years. The company is now servicing huge multinational and government organizations in India. Working on a few projects with him I realized that he used every moment of the time he spent with any of his employees very constructively. Most of us detest waiting outside client offices even when we are on time for the appointment, don't we? We either flip magazines or drink many glasses of water with nothing better to do. (Some lively salespeople also discuss the reception desk lady during this time!) I realized that this gentleman invariably struck a light conversation with his colleague every time he had to wait or drive long. On careful observation I noticed that this discussion was really not intended to be 'light'. It was always an opportunity for a great entrepreneur to motivate his teammates outside the formal hum of a boardroom. He would always discuss plans, shortcomings and goals with his colleague and ensure that even the waiting time was used for a critical responsibility he had to shoulder - the responsibility of continuously training his team.

As an organization head you will observe that there are times when even the most dedicated team members will show signs of fatigue or what they dangerously call 'burn-outs'. But this is nothing to get alarmed about. All of your teammates are human beings and the monotony of any single responsibility shows on many professionals in almost all organizations across the globe. However, how you tackle this recurring situation is what will pave the way for long-term employee relationships your company will form. Most human beings are in a way like automobiles. They run smooth and fast as long as they have fuel in their bellies. A regular dose of motivation and training ensures that the inferno within your young team remains alive along with continuous improvement in their professional competence. Also, after they have seen the turbulent times through they will need fewer lessons with every success and defeat of the company. They will finally be in a stage where they will be as driven as you are and will bear this torch for the next wave of professionals that will join your team in times to come.

> ***Box 9.*** *Ever wondered why Jack Welch has been accepted as one of the greatest management Gurus of contemporary times? No doubt he successfully led one of the most respected companies in the world. But the real reason behind his fame as a corporate genius was that his leadership nurtured leadership. Jack Welch never groomed employees to become only good workers or managers. He developed them into a powerful line of leadership.*
>
> *Today GE is a company stronger than ever not only because of its past, its huge size, corporate strength and powerful brand equity. It is stronger with the presence of magnificent leaders. And all because one man called Jack Welch made leadership at GE a part of life.*

I would like to reiterate that all this conversation about big companies and formal training should not bog you down. I insist that even if you are starting a two-member company (one apart from yourself) be equally zealous about the training period. A lot of entrepreneurs I have met fail to implement a lot of best practices simply because they lack the glamour or the cosmetics. Let me illustrate this with an example. An ex-colleague of mine who now runs a small market research outfit gets almost embarrassed when I suggest a monthly 'Star Performer' Award for his employees. This award should just have a token monetary value along with a certificate of excellence to convey the appreciation of the organization towards the team member who has given his or her best in that particular month. He loves the concept but refuses to implement it since he has only four members in his team. In his opinion such gestures suit only big companies that can select the best out of probably five hundred employees. In a small organization, he says, it all looks so artificial. Now the problem is not with the organization's size - it is with the mindset of the promoter. Remember, there is absolutely nothing that big companies do which you can't follow in your own humble yet honest way. Maybe the employees expect such recognition. You can also afford a small amount to ensure employee satisfaction. The good performers will become even better this way and the mediocre will try and run the extra mile to achieve this recognition. Everything is just perfect for my ex-colleague to announce this award. Everything except his own inhibitions.

The above example has been given just to convince you that value-driven activities are the same for all companies irrespective of their sizes. These must be implemented - with or without the glamour. So whether or not you can arrange for a conference room, refreshments and flashy looking trainers, the training exercise just has to be implemented. The reason why I am emphasizing this point so much is because I have seen cases where brilliant entrepreneurs fail to see this point and consider On-Job-Training to be the best solution. Of course it is a wonderful way of completing the training. But it should never replace or substitute serious instructor-led programs. In fact in our company we now ensure that not only every new entrant is subjected to a grilling training program, but it is also complimented with post-training examination and many hours with the senior management of the company. The training program and evaluation offer intense technical and operational education and the time spent with company seniors imbibes a feeling of belongingness and my favorite concept - collective dreaming!

HR Challenge and the 5 E Solution

If you remember I had mentioned earlier that when I am questioned on exactly what my responsibilities in the organization are, I reply "keeping people happy". This is exactly the point I am trying to drive at this juncture. As an entrepreneur and a business leader you will have to shoulder tremendous responsibility of managing people in different walks of business life. Although the set of these 'people' includes numerous associates and partners, the primary role you will play is of managing the internal workforce of your company. This is a critical aspect of entrepreneurship since the productive contribution and retention of your people will determine the success route of your organization right from the beginning. A manufacturing unit in New Delhi recently shut down simply because the Production Manager left the organization suddenly and the dependence of the organization on that one individual altered the destiny of that company. And with only a little experience you will realize how susceptible you and your organization can be to a similar situation. The reason is that being a new company you cannot afford to pay multiple people for the same role. Also, since you will have a very small workforce to begin with, every member of that team would be playing a mission critical role. This is an area all smart entrepreneurs need to watch out for.

But how will you be able to devote so much time and energy into this area when you also have innumerable other important things to look after including sales, collections, accounts, investor relations, operations and overall strategic direction? Bigger organizations have focused HR departments with professionals concentrating only on this area. You obviously can't hire an HR manager at this stage and thus the responsibility falls 100% on your shoulders. And with human beings being extremely complex living forms, is there a set of simple guidelines that we can follow and be reasonably competent human resource developers and managers? Honestly, there isn't. But I will sincerely attempt to simplify the situation by sharing with you what I have been following for the last few years - the 5 E solution.

The 5 E's practice is a HR 'formula for beginners'. And most of us are beginners till we have spent a decade in the industry and met and managed at least one thousand different individuals. The 5 E's go this way - Educate, Encourage, Evaluate, Empower and Enhance. As most business text, this is also a collection of some common sense. But again, as most management text, it will make you realize the simplicity only after you have read all of them.

1. **Educate** - Can you expect anyone to design a computer microchip without advanced education on hardware and software systems? Can a doctor operate on a patient's heart without formal training on cardiac surgery? Obviously not. Similarly, before any

contribution can be expected from a teammate, it is very important to educate him or her on the area of operations to be handled. Elaboration on this point would just be a repetition of what has been discussed in the previous topic.

2. **Encourage** - One of my relatives works as a Corporate Sales Manager with Idea Cellular, one of the leading mobile telephony services of India. On seeing him speak on the phone with his sales force I noticed a glaring variation. He almost used abusive language with some of the sales people working in his team and on the other hand used extremely appreciative words for the others. I asked him the reason for the same and he explained that there was no pardoning the seasoned and experienced sales force for poor performance but the newcomers should be praised even on failed sales attempts. "The newcomers need it to surge ahead relentlessly" he said. Although I do not agree with the unforgiving approach towards the experienced sales team, I am completely in sync with the management of the fresh recruits. The newly acquired workforce is like small plants that need a regular dose of water, fertilizer and pesticides. Once they reach the critical threshold size and mass, they can manage without all this well. So make it a point to pat shoulders whenever possible. On speaking to an executive from the UB Group in a train one day I discovered the closest representation for new human resource management. She explained elaborately to me that new workers should be treated like an Indian

potter controls a new vessel being created on a potter's wheel. You need to keep up the pressure from the top to give it the right shape - but support it from below every time it gets too much.

3. **Evaluate** - Every now and then you will stumble upon a situation when you need to understand the outcome of your efforts in training and developing your team along with the direct impact of every individual on the total productivity of your organization. And there is nothing wrong in this exercise since each member of your team, apart from being a value-creator, is also a serious cost center. Business sense demands that every resource deployed into the organization has to add value to the expected level or be further whetted or replaced. And this obviously includes the human resource of the organization. Especially if you are planning to launch a services company, wage bills will form the lion's share of your total costs. Even great companies like Infosys have Performance Improvement Programs for under-performing persons and is a practice followed by almost every organization I have interacted with. So be prepared to go in for appraisals for all your people in a planned and systematic way. There is nothing negative about this process and is an accepted norm of human resources evaluation and rewarding. Not only will this on-going system help you improve the collective performance of your team but also enable you to identify the shining jewels of your outfit. The next step of the 5 E's sequence would also be dependent on the successful implementation of this stage.

4. **Empower** - Remember Jack Welch? Or why go all that far at all. Even Dhirubhai Ambani, one of the biggest geniuses of corporate India was known to manage his vast empire with the assistance of his two brilliant sons and fifty lieutenants. Empowerment is one of the crying needs if you want your humble start-up to assume the size of a large corporation one day. A very wise man had once said 'A man may not know all that he can do, but he must know all that he can't'. With even basic understanding of business dynamics you would understand that you cannot possibly manage every arm, every department and every function of your company yourself and the ability to effectively delegate and empower your people will assist you in overcoming this shortfall. And don't wait for the 'departments' to actually get formed. Empowerment of your people is a culture that needs to be put in place right from day one. This will serve two purposes. One, it will make your company a more efficient organization and two; it will give your people the freedom to think, work and innovate. We are working with a big construction company in India's largest state where everything else seems okay except for the empowerment of people. Not even the senior most managers can issue even the smallest of payments to vendors and every letterhead to be printed needs the approval of the Managing Director. Such companies suffer heavily in today's fast track corporate sector and in the 'animal analysis' of companies I would place them as the Elephant - big but rigid, slow and top-heavy!

5. **Enhance** - During my internship with Philips India, I was working under the Regional Sales Manager for the domestic appliances division of the company. He was known to be a very hard taskmaster and was a nightmare for his salespeople. During one of my learning sessions in his cabin I happened to witness a sales management scene. One of the sales officers of the company had been performing badly for a few months and the Regional Manager had called him for an explanation. On being asked about the dismal performance the salesman almost broke down and narrated how he had been giving his best to the organization. He described how he was the salesman who spent maximum time on the field, had all his reports in place every evening before he left office, made calls to distributors everyday and how he was almost facing marital problems due to the minimal time he spent with his family. His side of the story sounded very genuine and I expected the RM to soften up a bit. On the contrary the RM asked him a simple question "So what happened at the end of all this effort? Where are the results?" This incident made me aware of one straight fact about the cruel world of business - performance is the only indicator of contribution to an organization and the only route to corporate growth. Obviously, as an outcome of your evaluation and empowerment, screen the real performers of the organization and enhance their responsibilities, compensation and spans of control. Remember, good workers need a constant acknowledgement from the Management of an organization in the simple forms of money, recognition

and power. Honestly, aren't these exactly what all of us want in one form or the other? This will be the last but recurring step in the simple yet very useful 5 E guidelines.

Rolling Out Your Sales Effort

Welcome to Hell! And trust me this is what your personal and professional life will become when you try and actually sell everything that you have been planning. Even for the people who have faced the sales fire before in life, the challenge in selling new products and new services from a new company to a new client will be an altogether different ballgame. Without sounding too discouraging, I would only emphasize that you will have almost no advantage on your side - no power brand, no track record, no experience, no relationships and no advertising of any kind to support you. Imagine, would you buy a product or service from a company if you discovered you were the first one to do so? Where will the credibility or just the ability of the company to deliver come from? This is exactly what will ensure that most of your first hundred sales calls would show absolutely no result. To state the truth, I had a few prospective customers who almost laughed at me when I told them they were the first ones!

So where does the solution lie? There just has to be a solution since all organizations must have closed their first few deals to become established companies of today. They must have found some way to reach and convince clients. If they can, so can we. Although I am a staunch believer that sales skills cannot be taught to anyone overnight and a book will certainly not do any wonders. However, please take a look at the suggestions that follow to gain some practical insights into how the tough road can be made comparatively smoother. All the points given below are completely based on practical experience and hundreds of mistakes made by us and a lot of other entrepreneurial ventures. You need not make these mistakes all over again and this text might help in preventing you from reinventing the wheel.

1. Write down a profile of your company even if there isn't really one in order. This takes you into the marketing and communications realm and majority of what most companies write in their communication media is just a glamorously worded presentation of not-so-impressive achievements. So even if you don't have clients and awards to talk about, conjure up some impressive content yourself or from sources around you without invading copyrights. (Websites of competitors can be an ocean of such info - but remember copyright issues). It may just be a few pages of your team profile, product specifications or even management text. Most of your customers will not read everything but a bundle of papers called your company profile will make bargains easier for you.

2. Just the way it was suggested that you try and raise investment from friends and relatives, the same principle applies in attempting to book your first few orders. Whether you are offering products and services to organizations or to individuals, the people who know you will be the most encouraging customers. For example if you are beginning work with a small investment consultancy, make sure that

your father, brother, uncle, friend and colleagues become your first set of clients. On the other hand, use your investors' (if any) contacts and network to look for angel customers.

3. References work like magic. Even if your immediate circle of friends and acquaintances do not fall within your target market, ask them for references (at least ten each). These will guide you to the right prospective buyers with a word of appreciation. My company bagged its first order from one of our investors' best friend.

4. Try and forge alliances and collaborations with organizations in related fields. For instance if you are in the business of manufacturing signage boards and visual merchandize, it might be a good idea to establish sales channels instead of trying to crack accounts directly. An advertising agency or a printing house would be ideal partners and can introduce you to their clients for a regular margin out of your revenue accruals from that account. These will not only kick-start a small stream of revenue for you but also provide you with a client portfolio and some crucial work experience.

5. A well-balanced pricing strategy plays an important role in determining the success of your sales effort. Frankly, you will have to crash your offer prices way below industry and competitor standards. A large number of Indian customers are extremely price conscious and would take the chance of working with newcomers if they were convinced of a good deal

having come by. This strategy may not give you desired profit margins but you must remember that your first goal should be to get clients and revenue streams in place. Work on a purely cost-covering basis and wait till your market presence, experience and repeat orders fetch you the profits. This may sound like a difficult proposition but you will agree that some money is better than no money at all.

6. Unlike established companies you will be grossly under-prepared to face difficult questions about product or service delivery. In fact you will be surprised at the amount of knowledge you will need right at the time of pitching if you are even in a remotely knowledge intensive business. There are numerous things that books and the Internet can never teach you about your business and will follow only after you have spent some sweat on the domain. Nevertheless, being in the position you are, it becomes even more critical to gather as much information and knowledge about your business as possible. With whatever domain insight you have, ensure that every call that your sales reps make are loaded with documents and papers. This becomes even more essential if you are in a services business. Services need tangible support and these brochures will offer just that. They may not be glossy printed papers and can be simple photocopies, but being equipped with them will make all the difference for your sales team.

7. Identify sectors or organizations that you need to reach out to during the first phase of your sales. Most

likely you will have a small sales force and limited resources. So pinpoint the areas you feel would deliver maximum results. This would give you the opportunity to research a target market segment and go for it in full steam. A haphazard sales approach has lower probability of showing immediate results. Here is an example. Suppose you have literary interest and you set up a small publication house. Now it would be important for you to understand that the book-trade is a very vast field and to succeed you need to make a mark as a publisher. The most fruitful approach should be to select any one area like Management, History, Cooking, Children Books, Defense or Fiction and address that target audience with a focused view. It would make more business sense for you to be called a great management books' publisher than a mediocre publisher of just any books.

8. The last but most effective rule - don't make sales based on the business sense of your prospective clients. Sell because you just have to! In my opening lines where I discussed the absence of any advantages for your start-up company, I skipped one of the biggest advantages you will always have - the undying aggression and energy of a start-up company! The fiercest sales efforts I have ever witnessed have all been stories from entrepreneurial ventures. Established organizations have tools like sales targets, rewards, incentives, statistics and charts to support their sales efforts. Start-ups have only one support system and that is the simple word called survival. I cannot explain it in words and you will not understand

right now. But you will see that your instinct for survival will be your biggest sales agent.

I really want all wannabe entrepreneurs to concentrate on the last point mentioned above. All the suggestions made before that can be figured out with comparative ease. However, this last bullet is what explains why some start-ups crash while the others become big corporations. Have you ever wondered why even in large organizations a majority of orders are booked within the last few days of the target achievement deadline? It is simply because of the pressure that gets built up by then and sales executives and managers have to report figures to their respective seniors. Now think about it. If the routine fear of a senior's displeasure can lead to better sales performance, what can the fear of losing a career do? And what can the fear of shattered dreams and failed ambitions do? When you are in the driver's seat and going crazy trying to sell, sell and sell against all possible odds and hardships, you will realize why a few pages back I had mentioned that start-ups thrive and survive on adrenalin.

So lead your sales force like a lion and lead by example. It has been accepted widely that sales people normally follow the footprints of their managers. An aggressive sales manager develops fiery sales executives and the chain just goes on. Imagine a situation where you have spent over twenty hours preparing a sales presentation. You visit a client ten times before he finally says yes or no and you make hundreds of phone calls without the fear of constant rejection. Trust me, most able sales professionals will follow suit - and that is exactly what your organization would need.

Some of you might be thinking as to how conveniently I have overlooked the role quality, efficiency and a product's value proposition play in sales and marketing. This observation is not wrong but I would emphatically state that this text does not aim to offer advice on some of the most obvious best practices in business. Quality matters, efficiency counts and the value proposition is critical. But these are accepted principles and I am assuming that you already understand all these. I am only trying to suggest how you can make the most of your sales effort irrespective of the product or service you intend to bring forward to the market.

Finally, I would like to clarify that despite all that I have mentioned, sales cannot be made only on sheer determination. You would be the best judge on how to add value to your products and services and how to really go about the marketing track. However, I am sure it will be endorsed whole heartedly by most successful entrepreneurs that energy, aggression, focus and an indescribable madness to sell goes a long way in promoting the revenue figures and overall market strength of a young company. And this is where the action is!

Work Environment

When you commence work with the people you have newly recruited you will realize that following rules is much simpler than framing them, blending into a work culture is easier than nurturing one and obviously pointing out shortcomings requires no effort as compared to managing them. Especially in a scenario where every move you personally make will lead to an invisible but potent 'trickle down' effect within your organization.

Study this example. We are working with an entertainment company that has built and managed many multiplex cinema halls in the country. While working on this assignment we happened to spend numerous hours in this organization. A startling revelation was the frequent use of expletives among the employees. People were used to abusing each other almost all the time, irrespective of where and with whom they were sitting. This was a disgusting experience for all our client servicing associates who were working on that project. Eventually, one day we discovered the source of this culture. In our meeting with the Chairman of that company at the time of project completion, we were shocked to see that he carried a perpetual bad temper and threw unbelievably poor language at even the highest Executive of his company. Though he spared us the delight of being at the receiving end of his pretty words, we left his Boardroom with a very bitter taste. And we realized that this bitterness had spread into his organization like a plague.

So what do you do to ensure that you are developing a happy and vibrant organization? A lot of tips on this issue would be offered in the last chapter of this book. At this juncture, make a note of the following suggestions -

1. Some things about the American way of working are really worth inculcating into your company. For example, the use of first names (nick names are even better) to address each other, including the CEO, is a brilliant practice. It brings about an ease of

interacting and lends an overall feel of zero-bureaucracy in the organization.

2. Even within the limited resources you may have, it is a good idea to bring together a bright and alive office. It takes nothing much really. Just a few humorous wall-posters, a few stress-busting toys and rich colors on the walls. This would make being in office a pleasant experience for your people and will make them like spending time at the workplace. However, this is a personal opinion and variations to this rule may exist based on the type of business you are in.

3. Organize pizza parties and courtyard cricket matches for your team. Remember, all work and no play makes Jack a very bored manager. So be responsive towards the 'living' needs of your team and allow them (in fact encourage them) to break free from mundane routines and participate in entertainment and team-building exercises. You will see how it will do wonders to the family spirit in the company and how colleagues will turn into friends.

4. Introduce the 'solution' approach into your people and not the 'problem' approach. You will see a lot of them walking up to you with innumerable problems. Don't be the solution provider - be just the facilitator. Ask everyone to think of a suggested solution before they report a problem. If feasible, ask them to implement it themselves. Here is an example. In our organization one of the Tech Associates came to me complaining about slow Internet connectivity in office. Being a technology services company,

bandwidth assumes critical importance. However, I refused to offer a solution and asked the Associate to figure one out within our resource allocation for connectivity and implement it in a week. In two days I had the latest service providers' catalogues and prices on my table and we quickly selected one of the choices. The importance does not lie in the size of the problem. It lies in nurturing a 'think-of-a-solution-and-implement-it-yourself' culture.

5. Be careful about the code of dressing you insist on. Let the customer facing people be dressed in formals and allow all the others to wear business casuals. There is no point in making a regimented organization when it does not really provide any serious value-add. Again, this is only a suggestion and you are the best judge to decide.

6. As far as possible, hold gatherings of your entire team whenever time and opportunity permit. It is very important to have your whole team involved in the day-to-day planning and the long-term intent of your company. This will not only induce transparency in your operations but also bring everyone into perfect communication levels with each other and into the mainstream of the organization.

As a thumb rule, keep the going happy and alive as far as possible. Everyone loves to work in a place that offers enough room for humor, laughter, friendship and communication. These are what I call 'operations catalysts' for a company that will enhance the overall productivity of your organization even before you notice it.

Keep reminding your people about the rules and disciplines of your organization but don't try and enforce them brutally. A lot of large companies are very strict with rules but they can afford to do that. They pay people much higher than you would along with offering the brand strength to them. But if you emulate the large corporations...God help your attrition rates! So this will demand a lot of managerial skills and you will have to engineer a good balancing act between the freedom you offer to your team and putting your foot down when situation forces you to.

Finally, keep a simple guideline for yourself and everyone around you - learn, implement and be committed, and have a lot of fun while doing all these!

Managing Cash Flow

Ever wondered why start-up businesspeople look stressed out almost all the time? Here's why. Imagine a situation where you need to pay rent, phone bills, salaries, installments, reimbursements and travel expenses in a week's time. The total money to be paid out amounts to USD 5000 or INR 2,40,000 approximately. Unfortunately your bank account reflects a total deposit of USD 300. With any substantial cash inflows seeming distant, would you not be stressed? It is as simple and as real as that!

One of the biggest impediments towards smooth business functioning and one of the most important skills you will have to learn in your entrepreneurial career is the buzzword called 'cash flow'. In fact if you assess business cycles carefully, you will realize that the essence of all corporate processes and operations lie in this deceptively simple term. And seasoned entrepreneurs are masters of this art. Cash flows effect all organizations equally, irrespective of their sizes and nature of work. No business can survive long without a regular supply of funds and nearly no amount of cash reserves can last beyond a few quarters at best. Moreover, real life business conditions will teach you that getting your fair dues in time is a utopian state and very few outstanding invoices are really cleared just when you deserve them. In fact during our first few months in business we never cared too much about the receivables. We honestly believed that once an order is delivered the compensation is our moral and professional right and will certainly come in at the agreed time. Unfortunately, our clients didn't think the same way. And slowly we realized that it was not just our clients who delayed payments...it was nearly a worldwide phenomenon. As an outcome, collections are now considered as important as sales, if not more.

But why is cash flow understanding considered such a big deal anyway? After all it's just balancing the money that comes in with what goes out, right? I wish it were that easy. I met a very impressive and knowledgeable bureaucrat a few months back. During a casual discussion he asked me how I ran a whole organization at such a young age. He stated very emphatically about himself that he can run the government of a whole country if need be, but cannot dream of managing even a small grocery store. The reason he cited was that he just failed to understand cash flow.

Professional cash flow management involves a lot more talent heads than you thought. It requires a powerful blend of financial management, forecasting capabilities, mathematics (oops!), logistics, risk management and prioritization.

A few cash flow tips only to make your ride less bumpy -

1. When you feel your expenses will be one dollar on any head, add twenty-five cents to it. When you think your earning will be one dollar, reduce twenty-five cents. This is a simple and age-old method used by the business community and in the absence of financial specialists and models this will keep you on a conservative and secure footing all the time.

2. Make your mind a simple calculator. It should be able to add and delete all the time and keep a mental note of bank reconciliation figures. In any case, this is something you would not have to work too hard on. You will just learn it with time.

3. Make it a habit to sit down with the accounts books every evening before you leave work. It will take only fifteen minutes of your time but give you a strong grip on all the inflows and outflows.

4. Make payment collections a part of your organization's work. This is a simple suggestion but has a lot of weight attached to it. It has almost become a standard that entrepreneurs lose a lot of money in the market before they learn the importance of effective collections. Learn from others' mistakes and keep an eye on collections from day one.

5. Hold on to your cash as long as you can. However

poor this may sound in social parlance, it has many benefits for a young, low-on-cash organization. But be very cautious in the way you prioritize the payment schedules. Utility bills like electricity, phones and rent has to be on topmost priority. The salaries of your team follow as an immediate second. The rest can be allocated on a pure need and necessity basis.

6. Make a conscious effort to forecast the revenues and costs at least a month in advance (this becomes three to six months as soon as your business reaches a certain scale and size). Forecasting will not only help you manage the money better, it will also spur you to achieve those targets.

Finally, I just have to mention that no one can really teach you cash flow management. This is a training that you will go through as you move ahead with your entrepreneurial career. And the advantage is that as you do that, the importance of every penny will increase for you with each passing day. That will be your greatest teacher.

The Final Frontier of your Start-Up Company

Building an organization for 100 years

My task is almost fulfilled. The fundamental objective behind writing this book was to give you a true and practical (even brutal at places) picture of the entrepreneurial journey. In other words, it was to offer you a handbook on how to build an organization from scratch. However, is the corporate sector or even life about reaching a particular destination and concluding the climb?

Or is it about an endless ascent and strife? There is still an important aspect screaming for our attention. It is an aspect that deals with the imperative thirst an entrepreneur needs to have for achieving infinite growth and impossible dreams. An aspect that deals with the principle that maintaining success is more difficult than achieving success once. As a corollary, which can be backed by hundreds of examples, managing and continuously developing a company is much tougher than creating one.

I happened to read a small study a few days back that pointed towards an astonishing revelation - great corporate founders have rarely been brilliant corporate managers. Of course we are excluding the likes of Bill Gates and Dhirubhai Ambani from this analysis as they are beyond any measurement management theory can ever set. However, on a more generalized pattern, it has been witnessed in several cases that organizations reach a plateau in terms of growth and it sometimes takes a generation change to bring back vibrance into the company. A management consultant once narrated to me the case of a senior corporate executive who was a renowned 'specialist' in building start-up companies. He had been a part of many start-ups that he steered towards stability and growth. Despite his contribution in the early stages of development, the management of each of these organizations invariably forced him to resign from the companies after he had completed a four to six year stint. This could not have been pure coincidence. What do you think could have been the reason? Obviously, his skill sets that were phenomenal in nursing young companies were not suited to manage them after they attained a certain scale and size. This is a very real threat many entrepreneurs face.

Also, it would be wrong to blame only the professional fabric of an entrepreneur for the stagnation threats an organization faces. Most business managers would agree that stagnation or falling into a 'growth trap' is a collective shortcoming of the organization and cannot be attributed to any one person or designation. However, being at the helm of affairs in your company and the original visionary, it becomes an unwritten responsibility of the entrepreneur to carve out the growth continuum for his or her company.

But what is it that really differs in the people who build great organizations and the people who manage them? How can we logically accept that someone who sows the very seeds of a start-up company can actually lose his or her grip on the development of the company as time passes? The answer lies in a simple analysis of the diametrically opposite approaches of management required while building an organization and when running an established company. For example, in a start-up company the top management has to break all rules to surge ahead. They have to introduce tremendous flexibility into the system to ensure optimal utilization of the limited resources the company may have. Work is normally completed on an ad hoc basis and the management actually encourages the employees to take initiative and offer quicker shorter routes without worrying too much about rules and systems. Functions see complete overlaps sometimes and the company almost runs on the 'one for all and all for one' principle. Although this is a vibrant work environment for a small young company looking only to keep moving, it can prove to be disastrous for a big and well-established company. Why? Simply because the adrenalin approach does not work well when the scale of operations and the number of people involved, both customers and employees, is much higher. In the latter case an organization has to bank on standards, systems, processes and procedures. It is next to impossible to run a company with many clients and many orders on a purely process-free structure. Consider a small software company with four to five clients and six to eight software developers. In such a scenario it is not only convenient but more sensible to let work flow on the basis of each individual's time schedule and availability. Also, deadlines can be kept in mind and projects can be stopped or started based on them. On the other hand imagine a software company with two hundred developers and fifty clients. It will be virtually impossible to manage the entire operations unless some standard procedures and project management techniques are used. Quality issues, timelines, testing and debugging, documentation and a whole lot of other areas would have to be addressed and that can be done only with some industry best-practices and procedural benchmarks in place. Now come back to the discussion on the management approaches of entrepreneurs. An entrepreneur would most probably start with the small scale of operations we mentioned in the example. With his or her drive and ability to pump in boundless energy into the team, the entrepreneur will successfully lead the company towards a profitable path and growth. However, this growth continues only till the time day-to-day operations and clients can be handled on an individual scrutiny level. The model for running the company changes drastically when the company goes beyond a certain threshold level of scale and size and the people of the company along with the management have to invent new and professional ways of managing this growth. It is exactly at this stage when entrepreneurs face the highest risk of managerial obsolescence. More often than not they continue to work on the same principles and models that they followed during the start-up stage. Moreover, being the architects of those models, it becomes even more difficult for them to accept the limited applicability of these models and let go of them at the right stage in their company's life cycle.

Here is another example. This deals with the human resource management of an organization. How does an entrepreneur manage his or her people and retain them even in the worst of times? This is an area we have discussed before and will find relevance under this topic. Most start-up business leaders are deeply connected to their immediate teams and enthuse them with drive and commitment through personal relations, a shared vision and regular communication. They follow complete transparency and minimal hierarchies. It is typical for an entrepreneur to gather together his or her small team in the event of a major decision or a crisis. These young organizations thrive on this participation and direct contact with the top management. What happens when these organizations grow in number? Will an entrepreneur be able to communicate equally well with one hundred employees as he or she did with five? Of course not. Which obviously means that the organization's human resource management has to go through a metamorphosis that entails the formal introduction of recruitment, appraisal and administrative policies - policies that most start-up business people are unaware of. As an outcome, the company becomes a haphazard combination of 'big company policies' and 'small company flexibility' thus leading to confusion in the overall HR dynamics. The desire and habit of an entrepreneur to manage the team through personal relations becomes unfair to most team members since the direct observation of and mind-space allocation to each individual becomes virtually impossible. This causes judgmental and ill-informed decisions leading to severe dissatisfaction amongst the people. Even in a case where the entrepreneur creates HRM standards and develops a formal personnel department, some handicaps continue to exist. With the introduction of middle management in the company, the single most crucial edge of an entrepreneur is also lost - that is the ability to drive people beyond all logic only through personal example and charisma. Entrepreneurs now have to depend on management hierarchies to send their message and philosophy across to every member of the organization. And this is something they have probably not been accustomed to. On the other hand, brilliant managers have the skill to keep the entire organization committed by effective delegation and management of people through people.

The aforementioned examples highlight the tremendous change that a start-up company goes through as it moves ahead on its growth curve. It becomes imperative for an entrepreneur to change management techniques and methodologies and evolve with the organization. It is at this phase in your business that you would have to come back to the existing schools of management thought and run your company on widely accepted business practices. I resist myself from discussing various areas of keen importance as they do not fall within the scope of this book. You will find several sources of knowledge when you reach this point in your entrepreneurial life and then you would probably have to graduate from reading 'Build From Scratch' to reading 'Built to Last', the brilliant book on corporate strategy, growth and longevity.

The transition would not be an issue at all for those who have many valuable years of experience behind them before they jumped on to the entrepreneurial bandwagon. For example, Ashok Soota created MindTree, the well known IT services company, after he had headed two large corporations. Obviously, his experience and knowledge would overcome any possible hurdles on the way of MindTree's growth. But for those of you who are still very young in the corporate society, the willingness and attitude to enhance your own skill set along with the scale and size of your company will be critical for the long-term success of your organization. From pure play sales and survival management you will move into the realm of customer relations, process implementation and brand management. And all this would offer you the same level of excitement that your first day at your office or factory did. In fact, this is the most wonderful aspect of entrepreneurship.

* * * * * * * * *

With this we come to a conclusion of the discussion we have had over the last couple of hundred pages. The very fact that you have read so far without losing your focus on this topic is in itself a powerful indicator of your patience, eagerness and more than just an interest in the world of start-up businesses. It is a good sign. It is now that you have to spend a few days with yourself and do some internal analysis. I repeat something that I mentioned a few pages back - do not get too bogged down with only thinking and planning. If you are determined to build a life around your ambitions and not just pure need, some reliance on your gut feel is absolutely essential. Decisions like these can never just be logical and defined. They always involve a factor of personal desire.

A word of caution at this stage. Keeping all that I have said in the previous pages and chapters in mind, be very careful before you pull the plug on your existing occupation. This is especially for those who have many responsibilities and a strong need for a regular paycheck. I emphasize once again that starting your own enterprise is not as risky as it sometimes seems to be, but gestation periods and time-lags between sowing and reaping certainly exist. But for those of you who have age on your side and comparatively lower levels of responsibility, do not wait too long. I have known many people who discuss their plans to start their own company every time they sit and drink with their friends. And they have been doing this for the last five to six years. And what are you really waiting for anyway? No one will ever come to you with a few million dollars and a great business idea and request you to take the initiative. You will have to work your way to it. For anyone who wishes to discuss his or her business plan with me, I would be very happy to assist. For more information, consultancy, white papers and my contact numbers, please log onto the website of this book (the URL is given on the cover of the book).

I sincerely hope that this book has proven to be of some help to all its readers. I also pray that one day this book, in its humble position, is able to inspire another Dhirubhai or Henry Ford. What else can an author ask for!

Your company will be like the ship that is under your captaincy. If the ship hits rough waters the captain is the last one to remain on board, fighting to keep his vessel afloat. If the vessel goes down, a lot of captains go down with it. On the other hand, successful ventures of this ship would just ensure that you are the one right on top... with recognition, money, power and fame. This is why I sometimes say - there is no ship like entrepreneurship!

All the very best!

What NOT To Do In Your Young Company - *The 20 Point List*

1. No order is yours till you get the advance cheque, no money is received till it gets transferred into your account and no employee is recruited till he shows up half hour early on the joining date. **Do NOT count your chickens before they hatch!** Don't ever overestimate projected revenue and never underestimate costs. This will always allow you to be on a secure cash position. In other words, try and avoid expenses that you may make based on expected receivables. You will be surprised to witness how many such 'expected' payments get delayed (or bad!) by months.

2. **Do not overspend on advertising.** Marketing expenditure is the quickest and surest way of burning through your cash in no time. Even if your business is advertising intensive, be very careful in selecting the agency and the media.

3. **Never rebuke an employee** in the presence of other colleagues. This is one of the fundamental teachings of HR Gurus. However, in my opinion, break this principle whenever you identify a team member who is the epicenter of unhealthy organizational politics.

4. Even if you yourself are a chain smoker, **insist on your workplace being a no-smoking zone.** Allowing people to light cigarettes inside office premises displays poor corporate etiquettes and is a serious nuisance for the non-smokers. A point as basic and

simple as this is being mentioned here only after I witnessed numerous young offices practicing unbridled smoking in the garb of keeping the office 'alive'.

5. **Avoid the use of casual language** within your team. Remember, your organization will take the shape of the mould you provide.

6. **Don't ever behave like the owner** of the company (if you are running a 'limited' company, you wont be the owner anyway). Always take the role and behavior of a CEO or Chief Facilitator. You must understand that most people want to work for a company and not an individual.

7. **Don't ever let your office become a 'party zone'.** A lot of times when you bag a big order or when you suddenly collect a lot of money, some of your teammates may suggest a beer evening at office. In my opinion, treat your workplace like a temple. Take the team out for beer, but let the sanctity of your office remain untouched. It is only years later that you will realize the benefits of this discipline.

8. **Don't keep yourself last on the salary list.** It is a common tendency among entrepreneurs to believe that they have no professional or moral right to withdraw money from the company's account till they have settled some more pressing expense heads. This is a flawed approach. You must make it a point to pay yourself before you pay anyone else - no salaries, no bills, no fees. There are some deep-rooted reasons

behind this. Firstly, with the resource constraint that you would be working with, paying yourself last would almost mean never paying yourself. Secondly, it is human tendency that external pressures to raise money from the market (e.g. the threat of your phone lines being disconnected) are much stronger than your own need to do so. So you may not push yourself over the edge for your own salary but you will do it to keep the phones working. As a result, you will just work towards earning more revenue.

9. **Do not try and 'deep-dive' into every process** and every order of the organization. Learn to delegate responsibility and authority and you will see the organization becoming a much more efficient machine. Obviously, this rule cannot be implemented for the first few months when you have to proactively intervene and get the standard operating procedures in place.

10. **Never hide information** from your key people. Some of your accountants may suggest a careful screening of financial information. Although this is not completely wrong, try and share as much with the second tier of leadership in your organization as possible. Remember, complete transparency leads to complete trust.

11. **Never bite more than you can chew** when it comes to picking up orders. Although it is important to push the bar a little higher every time you go out to gather work, it is equally important to understand the resources you will have to plug in to fulfill those

commitments. I have seen complete decimation of some companies that could not deliver assignments and eventually lost millions.

12. **Stop people from playing computer games in office.** This may sound like regimentation but you will realize that hours can be wasted easily if you don't put a stop to it. Pornography obviously is a big threat that you need to guard against.

13. **Do not keep a distance from your people.** A lot of business owners I know purposely engineer a gap between the employees and themselves. This not only restricts communication but also damages their allegiance to you.

14. Try and **stop the formation of small informal groups** within your team. This would become impossible when your company assumes a bigger scale and size, but guard against it till your team is small. Your initial set of team members should be one big team and one big group. This way you will drastically cut down all chances of organizational politics creeping into your young and fragile company.

15. **Do not forget your investors** under any circumstances. If you are working with passive individual investors you will be very prone to get involved in day-to-day business pressures and overlook their presence on many occasions. This could be dangerous! You need to remember that even if the investors have transferred all the money to you and are not questioning you aggressively, they would

be watching you closely from a distance. Even otherwise, they were instrumental in nurturing your company when it needed it most and you owe a lot to them.

16. There is a popular saying originating from the North Indian business community - 'Gussa khaya, maal paraya'. This simply means - **loose your temper, loose your money**! Getting angry is not an option for entrepreneurs. No anger at clients, no anger at employees at certainly none at your investors. We at our Company have learnt the truth behind this statement only after some unfortunate experiences. Losing your cool would just make you more vulnerable and take away your entire professional aura. Eventually, you just lose the very money you are working and fighting for. Even in the worst of times, be stern, assertive but never aggressive.

17. **Don't be ruthless in putting performance pressure** on your sales people. It is very possible that the pressure on you to earn revenue gets passed on multifold to your sales team. Keeping the sales force aggressive is different from resorting to high-pressure tactics to convert orders. Make the sales team completely accountable but remember that the going will be tough for them too. They would be trying to sell products and services of an unknown company to completely unknown customers.

18. **Don't try and lead everyone by example every time.** You cannot always be the first one to enter office, write all the reports, not take any holidays and leave

office the last. It is good to give your initiative your best, but don't try and be superhuman. Moreover, your team has to learn to be responsible and disciplined even in your absence.

19. **Do not compromise with your health.** This may sound like a grandmotherly advice to you, but it is of utmost importance. Remember, your ability to work fourteen hours everyday will be your biggest asset and even a three-day stretch of illness can lead to severe losses. So take your meals on time, get good sleep and keep yourself as entertained as possible.

20. **Never lose sight of your goals** and never get disheartened. There will be several occasions when you feel everything is going wrong. Just don't forget, it really is the darkest before dawn.

* * * * * * * * * * * * *

India Research Press is a collectively run book publisher with support of Authors and Editors. Since our founding in 1999, we have tried to meet the needs of readers who are exploring, or are committed to the politics of change.

Our goal is to publish books that encourage critical thinking and constructive action on the key political, cultural, social, economic and ecological issues shaping life in the Indian Sub-continent and in the world. In this way, we hope to give expression to a wide diversity of democratic and social movements.

India Research Press publishes Original works-as well as-works under Rights with various University and Academic publishers throughout the world.

Since our conception, we have added two new imprints to our existing line of Academic publishing.The Group now has three seperate divisions & editors for its publishing programme and many new titles, scheduled in the coming months. The India Research Press also has New Overseas Distributors for the sale of its titles in the USA and the European continent. The group is proud to introduce its three divisions of publishing.

Academic Publishing Division.

General Division – Mass Market including Fiction.

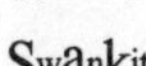

General Division – Health, Non Fiction and Educational titles.

The group is headed by Anuj Bahri Malhotra, its CEO & Commissioning Manager. He is assisted by an efficient and professional staff of Editors, Administrator, Office Assistants and Accountant. Born to a bookseller's family, running the most sought after bookshop [Bahri Sons] in the country, Anuj has a long 23 years experience in the Indian Book Industry.

India Research Press is a multi-disciplinary book publisher with support of Authors and Editors. Since our founding in 1999, we have tried to meet the needs of readers who are expecting [illegible] committed to the political elections.

Our goal is to publish books that encourage critical thinking and constructive action on the key political, cultural, social, economic and ecological issues shaping life in the Indian Sub-continent and in the world. In this way, we hope to give expression to a wide diversity of democratic and social movements.

India Research Press publishes original works as well as works under Rights with various University and Academic publishers throughout the world.

Since the inception, we have added two new imprints to our existing line of Academic publishing. The Group now has three separate divisions & almost ... its publishing programme and many new titles scheduled in the coming months. The India Research Press also has New Overseas Distributors for the sale of its titles in the USA and the European countries. The group is proud to introduce its three divisions of publishing:

Academic Publishing Division

General Division – Mass Market including Fiction

General Division – Health, Non Fiction and Motivational titles

The group is headed by Mr. Ajay Pratap Malhotra, the CEO & Managing Director. He is assisted by an efficient and professional staff of Editors, Administration Officer, Assistants and Accountant. Born to a Booksellers family, running the most successful book shop (Bahri Sons) in the country, Ajay has a long 25 years experience in the Indian Book Industry.